THE FACTS ABOUT ENDOMETRIOSIS

DID YOU KNOW:

- Endometriosis is hard to diagnose because it resembles so many other conditions, including flu, fibroid tumors, irritable bowel syndrome, and pelvic inflammatory disease

- Endometriosis is not caused by stress

- Women who have had one or two children are just as likely to develop endometriosis as those who have never given birth

- Caucasian, black, and Asian women, thin or heavyset, from any economic group, housewives or career women—all are just as likely to develop endometriosis. There is no typical endometriosis patient.

Hope and help are now available. Now you can seek expert medical help and break the pattern of pain and discomfort. You'll find everything you need to know in . . .

WHAT WOMEN CAN DO ABOUT CHRONIC ENDOMETRIOSIS

THE DELL MEDICAL LIBRARY:

RELIEF FROM CHRONIC BACKACHE
RELIEF FROM CHRONIC HEADACHE
RELIEF FROM CHRONIC TMJ PAIN
RELIEF FROM CHRONIC ARTHRITIS PAIN
LEARNING TO LIVE WITH CHRONIC IBS
LEARNING TO LIVE WITH
CHRONIC FATIGUE SYNDROME
WHAT WOMEN CAN DO ABOUT
CHRONIC ENDOMETRIOSIS
WHAT YOU CAN DO ABOUT INFERTILITY
WHAT WOMEN SHOULD KNOW ABOUT MENOPAUSE
WHAT YOU CAN DO ABOUT DIABETES

What Women Can Do About Chronic
ENDOMETRIOSIS

Judith Sachs

Foreword by Herbert Jaffin, M.D.

A LYNN SONBERG BOOK

Note: Medical science and endometriosis research are constantly evolving. Although every effort has been made to include the most current data in this book, there can be no guarantee that this information won't change with time and further research. The reader should bear in mind that this book is not for the purpose of self-diagnosis or self-treatment and that any and all medical problems should be referred to the expertise of appropriate health-care providers.

Published by
Dell Publishing
a division of
Bantam Doubleday Dell Publishing Group, Inc.
666 Fifth Avenue
New York, New York 10103

ISBN: 0-440-20646-4

Printed in the United States of America
Published simultaneously in Canada

June 1991

10 9 8 7 6 5 4 3 2 1

OPM

CONTENTS

CONTENTS

ACKNOWLEDGMENTS

I would like to express my thanks to the following for their time, expertise, information, advice, encouragement, and moral support:

Herbert Jaffin, M.D., Department of Obstetrics and Gynecology, Mount Sinai Hospital, New York, New York

Scott Eder, M.D., Department of Obstetrics and Gynecology, Princeton Medical Center, Princeton, New Jersey

Mary Lou Ballweg, Executive Director, Endometriosis Association

Nancy Petersen, R.N., St. Charles Medical Center, Bend, Oregon

Robert Breitstein, M.D., Beekman Downtown Clinic, New York, New York

Lucius Clay, M.D., Princeton Medical Center, Princeton, New Jersey

Rona Silverton, M.S.W., C.S.W., psychotherapist, Beekman Downtown Clinic, New York, New York

Paul Bahder, M.D., Princeton Homeopathy Clinic, Princeton, New Jersey

John Urich, Lawrenceville Acupuncture Center, Lawrenceville, New Jersey

Pat Schwartz, Bucks County (Pennsylvania) Endometriosis Support Group

and

All the women struggling with endometriosis who are learning more about how to help themselves manage the disease every day.

FOREWORD

Thanks to the tireless work of many committed men and women in research and clinical practice, endometriosis is far easier to diagnose and treat today than it ever was before. Although we still don't understand why this malfunction of the hormonal and immune systems plagues certain women, we are certainly closer to understanding it now than when I first went into practice twenty-eight years ago.

The most recent research has exploded many of the myths about the condition. It was previously assumed that endometriosis was the "career woman's disease" and that it occurred only in white, middle-class, childless patients. Evidence has clearly shown, however, that endometriosis can affect any woman of any age, race, or economic background.

Another prevalent myth was that most women who have endometriosis are infertile. We now know that this is simply not the case. Thanks to advanced hormonal manipulation, it is possible for almost any woman to conceive and bear children at any stage of the disease.

The worst symptom of endometriosis for most sufferers, of course, is monthly pain. In the past this pain severely hampered work and daily activity; it made sexual intercourse difficult or impossible. But thanks to today's diagnostic and therapeutic management techniques, both surgical and hormonal, pain can be reduced or even obliterated.

Today, minimal endometriosis can be managed with birth control pills, and more severe cases with the drugs danazol and GnRH. These extraordinary hormonal suppressants have proved to be greatly beneficial to thousands of women who must live with this disease. Innovative surgical techniques, too, have brought both diagnosis and treatment to new levels of sophistication.

Any disruption of normal reproductive functioning can cause stress. It can interrupt the flow of daily life, and it can put a strain on work, family, and social relationships. But the good news is that endometriosis patients are now getting the best care and the most attention they've ever received. In my years at Mount Sinai Hospital in New York City, I have treated hundreds of patients, most of whom have been able to cope with their symptoms and have children if they so desire.

In this excellent book, *What Women Can Do About Chronic Endometriosis,* Judith Sachs offers a complete picture of endometriosis. She gives an overview of the theories surrounding the disease and explains its various symptoms. She provides a complete description of the complex process of definitive diagnosis, which is possible only by means of laparoscopy and subsequent biopsy. She explains the various hormonal and surgical treatments currently in use.

This reassuring manual also provides practical information about advances in infertility treatment. It concisely previews an infertility workup and discusses the new procedures of in vitro fertilization—embryo transfer (IVF/ET) and gamete intrafallopian transfer (GIFT).

I found this book helpful and informative because it explains what a woman can do on her own to remain in control of her own physical and emotional well-being. One of the most crucial elements in the diagnosis and treatment of endometriosis is a trusting relationship between patient and doctor. This book encourages women to seek the very best medical care available, and it tells them how to find it. It also discusses the importance of emotional support from family and friends, as well as from groups of women who may also have the disease.

The cure for endometriosis may be forthcoming in the next ten years. Until such a breakthrough is found, it is essential for each patient to understand that she is entitled to the best medical care possible. Endometriosis can be managed, it can be treated, and there are remissions. Using the guidelines offered by this book, every woman with endometriosis can take steps to improve her health and the quality of her life.

HERBERT JAFFIN, M.D.
Senior Attending Obstetrician/Gynecologist,
    Mount Sinai Hospital
Associate Clinical Professor,
    Mount Sinai School of Medicine, New York, New York

INTRODUCTION

If you suffer from premenstrual and menstrual pain, if sexual intercourse is painful or even physically impossible for you, or if you cannot manage to get pregnant, you may have endometriosis. In this chronic disease, tissue displaced from the lining of the uterus grows on other organs of the body and interferes with their proper functioning.

In the past fifteen or twenty years, endometriosis has come to the forefront of Americans' awareness of gynecological issues. Thanks to the persistent research done by physicians and the media attention brought to the disease by women's groups, many more people now know about this chronic disease. Although it is still not completely understood and still makes life very difficult for many who suffer from it, endometriosis is diagnosable, treatable, and above all, manageable.

This book will help you to understand the symptoms that have puzzled and distressed you and perhaps even your physician. The various chapters explain the theories about why endometriosis occurs in certain women and takes you step by step through the various diagnostic procedures and therapeutic treatments, both surgical and pharmacological. The book also details the various emotional components and coping strategies you need to deal with your condition. Because the disease can and does affect women at all stages of life, a chapter is devoted to endometriosis in teenagers and older women.

The book also discusses alternative therapies and methods of pain management and pain reduction, such as diet and exercise, acupuncture, biofeedback, and homeopathy. The goal is for you to become a better-informed patient and therefore an asset to your physician in your treatment.

Although endometriosis is hard to treat and is often recurrent, it is not a life-threatening disease. Regardless of how extensive your condition is, there is only a very slight chance that your endometrial implants will become malignant. With proper diagnosis, conservative surgery, and possible follow-up drug therapy, you can hope to live a pain-free existence and conceive and carry a baby to term.

Until recently, the physical symptoms and emotional ramifications of endometriosis were often misunderstood and downplayed by the medical community. Only a few years ago, a woman who complained to her doctor that she had terrible menstrual pain might be told to buck up and deal with it, to go home and "get pregnant," to have a hysterectomy, or to see a psychotherapist for psychosomatic symptoms. Many endometriosis sufferers spent years doubting themselves because they could get no one—least of all their families and physicians—to trust their own judgment about their own bodies.

There are still many women who have no idea what endometriosis is. They only know that they are mystified by and hurting from monthly pain, sexual discomfort, and infertility. This book encourages them to seek help.

If you've already been diagnosed with endometriosis, you will be relieved to know that you are in very good company. More than five million American women have also been diagnosed with the condition. Now, not only can you get access to the very best medical care, you can find the backup you need from groups of women who share your problem. All over the country, endometriosis support groups meet on a regular basis to share medical information and give emotional sustenance.

Your primary source of relief, however, is your doctor. Together with him or her, you can create an alliance of trust and shared knowledge. By participating actively in your own treatment, you will find the best ways to manage your disease.

HOW DO YOU KNOW IF YOU HAVE ENDOMETRIOSIS?

Endometriosis comes from the Greek *endo*, meaning "inside," and *metri*, derived from *metra*, or "uterus." *Osis* means "an abnormal condition." The disease was named in 1921 by Dr. John Sampson, who showed that islands of endometrial tissue that were growing *outside* the uterus could cause pain and infertility. But endometriosis is not a new disease. Descriptions of the condition date back to the ancient Egyptians and Chinese.

The three most common symptoms of endometriosis are:

· increasing premenstrual and menstrual pain

· pain during intercourse

· infertility

You may experience all or none of these symptoms, or you may have many others that seem vaguely related to your menstrual cycle. Medical science has long known that endometriosis depends on the fluctuations of the estrogen and progesterone levels in the body, but the latest research in the field makes it increasingly clear that the immune system plays an equally large part in the inception and recurrence of the disease.

If you have endometriosis, or if you think you may have it, you may be enormously frustrated by the effort it takes to get a proper diagnosis. It's common female lore that monthly periods are *supposed* to be uncomfortable, causing cramps, bloating, and occasional gastrointestinal symptoms like constipation, diarrhea, or nausea. These symptoms occur so often in so many women that few bother to ask their doctor whether something might be really wrong. But *increasing monthly pain that begins prior to the first day of bleeding and that continues through your period is one of the most important indicators in the early detection of endometriosis.*

If you are in so much pain and discomfort that you cannot keep up your daily activities or your school, job, or exercise routines, it's time to have your problem investigated. The sooner you get help from an experienced health-care practitioner, the sooner you can begin to manage your endometriosis.

This disease is exceptionally elusive and complex; many of its facets are often hard to identify. With the knowledge you'll gain from this book and other sources, you can work together with your doctor to find a treatment that works for you.

A CASE HISTORY

Jill was an active, athletic child who started menstruating at the age of eleven. At first her periods were infrequent, but after a year or two, she settled into a twenty-seven-day cycle with a menstrual flow that lasted about a week. She typically had heavy bleeding on days three through five of her period. Over the years some months would be okay, but others would be terrible—she would lose so much blood that she felt faint.

Usually, her periods arrived right on time, but she learned

that emotional or physical stress could alter her cycle—accelerating or delaying it.

When she reached her mid-teens, she noticed that her cramping and discomfort were getting worse. Her discomfort now started several days before she bled instead of on the first day of her cycle. The pain was incapacitating at times, making her feel weak, dizzy, and nauseated, keeping her from extracurricular activities and after-school jobs. She talked to her mother and older sister about her symptoms. They both told her that yes, rotten cramps ran in the family. She would just have to learn to live with them.

When she was nineteen, she fell in love with a co-worker on her college newspaper, and they went to bed together. She found intercourse excruciating, but she figured that was because she was nervous and worried about getting pregnant. Her boyfriend soon grew tired of her excuses, and they broke up. Over the next few years, she had no sexual life at all, but her monthly cramps grew worse. It was agonizing just to move her bowels during her periods.

The next year, she met Larry. They were married after an eight-month courtship, during which she found that sex didn't hurt as much if she was on top. It wasn't great, but she could tolerate it. Larry stopped using condoms after they were married, but she never got pregnant. She went to a gynecologist to find out why, but the instant the doctor began the internal exam, she shrieked in pain and nearly jumped off the table. The doctor shook his head and asked if she'd ever heard of endometriosis.

THE MENSTRUAL CYCLE

Before we can understand Jill's pain and difficulty getting pregnant, it's necessary to talk a little about how the hormonal cycle works and how endometriosis can affect a woman's entire system.

Each month, your brain sends hormonal signals to your ovaries. The brain's hormones are gonadotrophin-releasing hormone (GnRH), follicle-stimulating hormone (FSH), and luteinizing hormone (LH). These hormones relay messages to the ovaries, which then produce their own hormones—estrogen and progesterone.

These hormones, released in fluctuating patterns, help to stimulate the production and release of an egg (which, if fertilized by a sperm, would develop into a fetus). They also prepare the lining of the uterus (the endometrium) for implantation and growth of that egg. If a sperm doesn't fertilize the egg, hormone levels fall in the body. The endometrial lining—which consists of tissue, blood, mucus, and various vaginal and cervical secretions as well as the remains of the egg—passes out of the body through the vaginal canal.

Endometriosis and the Menstrual Cycle

The endometrium grows, gets thicker, then is shed in accordance with the fluctuating influence of hormones during your monthly cycle. But if you have endometriosis, something else also occurs as this cycle progresses. Sometimes not all the menstrual debris sloughs off when you have your period. Some of it remains in your body, and it travels to a variety of sites outside the endometrium—the ovaries, the fallopian tubes, even the bowel or bladder.

In women with endometriosis, this tissue implants itself and grows. These implants respond to monthly hormonal changes just as the endometrium does: they swell as they become engorged with blood, then scar over as the hormonal levels fall. The implants have no passage out of the body as the endome-

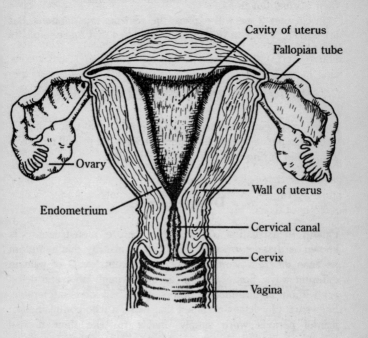

Figure 1　Female reproductive organs
(clockwise from top right: cavity of uterus, fallopian tube, wall of
uterus, cervical canal, cervix, vagina, endometrium, ovary)

trial lining does, which means that they can build up month
after month. These implants, which may be as small as tiny
dots or as large as grapefruits, can cause pain and scarring.
They may become large pelvic masses or weblike bands of

adhesions that glue the internal organs together and obstruct their normal function.

In Chapter 2 we will explore the reasons this happens, but for now, let's look at the physical problems that these implants can bring on.

PROBLEMS ENDOMETRIOSIS CAUSES

As we have seen, the three major symptoms that would make a doctor suspect a woman has endometriosis are painful menstruation, pain during intercourse, and infertility.

Dysmenorrhea

Painful menstruation, or pain just before menstruation, is known as *dysmenorrhea*. It's difficult to classify this symptom because different women react to different levels of pain in different ways. Some women can get through labor and delivery without medication; for others, a stubbed toe is intolerable. For years, physicians assumed that women who complained of painful periods were simply unable to take their normal monthly hormonal changes in stride. Many physicians interpreted the problems that often accompanied women's pain— nausea, dizziness, headaches, and lower back pain—as psychosomatic.

Not all endometriosis causes dysmenorrhea. Some women come into their doctors' offices with huge pelvic masses but have absolutely no discomfort at all. Others have minimal stages of the disease but are in exquisite pain for a good part of every month. This is because the implants tend to be more painful when they are located right next to a nerve ending, regardless of how large they are. An implant can be microscopic—barely a blip on the peritoneum—or it can be a huge, blood-filled cyst as large as a grapefruit.

Dyspareunia

Dyspareunia means "painful intercourse." During the sexual act, penile thrusting—particularly in the male-dominant position—moves the uterus around gently within the pelvic cavity. But if endometrial adhesions have fixed the uterus in place, even penetration may be agonizing. The pain can be particularly bad during your menstrual period when the implants are swollen and bleeding.

Large *endometriomas* (cysts of endometrial tissue that grow on the ovary) may become compressed during intercourse, which can be excruciating. But even the smallest implants, depending on their location, can cause pain. Spot bleeding may occur after intercourse, caused by thrusting that bruises or damages the implants.

The reason Jill tended to have less pain when she was on top of her husband was that her uterus had a slight amount of play in this position. When she was on top, she could move away from the deep penetration that stretched or traumatized the areas covered with endometrial implants.

Infertility

Infertility is the third symptom of endometriosis. Thirty to 40 percent of all women with "endo," as it's commonly called, are infertile. In the general population of women of childbearing age, only 15 percent are infertile. Of all infertile women, about one-third have been diagnosed with endometriosis. But endometriosis alone doesn't cause infertility. It's probably only one of several interrelated factors.

If endometrial implants are blocking the fallopian tubes or ovaries, or if the organs are twisted out of place by adhesions, the egg may not be able to make its normal passage out of the follicle and down the tube to the uterus. A variety of biochemical factors may also come into the picture. (For a full discussion, see Chapter 7.)

COULD IT BE SOMETHING ELSE?

Endometriosis is a difficult disease to diagnose. Its symptoms may be confused with symptoms of other diseases. Some doctors haven't seen a sufficient number of cases that they can recognize the groupings of symptoms and make a sure diagnosis, and even physicians who are familiar with the disease may have trouble identifying it in every patient.

The following medical conditions may be suspected instead of endometriosis:

Pelvic inflammatory disease (PID) can produce many of the same symptoms as endometriosis. To physicians who haven't seen many cases of endo, the pain and the adhesions on the pelvic organs might seem like symptoms of PID. But PID is quite different.

PID is an inflammation that results from the effects of a sexually transmitted disease, like chlamydia or gonorrhea, or from an infection caused by intolerance to an IUD. The longer these infections remain untreated, the higher the risk of damage to tubes and ovaries and the greater the likelihood that infertility will result. But if treated early, PID responds well to antibiotics. If you're being treated for PID but the antibiotics aren't helping, you and your physician may have misdiagnosed the problem.

Premenstrual syndrome (PMS) is often mentioned when a woman complains of pain before her period begins. Actually, PMS is a *mid*-cycle phenomenon. It occurs in women who are extremely sensitive to the monthly fluctuation of their hormones. PMS may cause pain, bloating, and severe depression.

Fibroid tumors are benign growths in or on the muscular wall of the uterus. A woman may have one large fibroid or many small ones. They can generally be detected in an internal exam. Small fibroids don't usually cause pain, but a large one can displace other organs, bringing on backaches, constipation, stress incontinence, heavy menstrual flow, or the passing of blood clots.

Ectopic pregnancy occurs when the egg is fertilized *outside* the uterus—most typically in one of the fallopian tubes. The kind of pain that this dangerous condition creates can be mistaken for the pain of endometriosis. If you have missed a period or have been spotting and feel that you may be pregnant, tell your doctor at the examination. An ectopic pregnancy must be treated immediately, or your tube could rupture, presenting a life-threatening situation. A pregnancy test and an ultrasound, as well as an internal exam, will usually make it possible for your physician to distinguish an ectopic pregnancy from endometriosis.

Irritable bowel syndrome or *spastic colon* can be confused with endometriosis of the rectum, bowel, or sigmoid colon. Implants in these locations produce chronic gastrointestinal symptoms.

Gas or *the flu* might be diagnosed when endometriosis causes symptoms such as nausea, vomiting, and chills.

Achiness, chronic lower back pain, bloating, fatigue, and general discomfort that comes and goes are typical symptoms of endometriosis. Unfortunately, they are the vague sort of ailments that make many doctors shrug and prescribe aspirin or even a mild antidepressant. Although these symptoms can be stress-related, they can also be symptoms of endometriosis—

particularly if they recur frequently. A thorough physical exam is very important.

A *psychosomatic origin* for menstrual pain can never be completely ruled out, but a sensitive physician will do a thorough medical history as well as a physical exam to be sure. He or she may ask you pointed questions to uncover any deeply rooted fears you may have about femininity, childbearing, or bleeding. If a doctor tells you "the pain is all in your mind," get a second opinion. Although having a chronic illness can be emotionally devastating, endometriosis is a medical condition with real physical symptoms.

If you have a symptom or symptoms that *could* indicate a problem other than endometriosis, there is one crucial element that must be examined. That is whether the symptom occurs around the time of your period. If your pain and discomfort are always significantly worse before and during your period, you and your physician should investigate further to see if you have endometriosis.

BUT DOESN'T EVERY WOMAN HAVE CRAMPS?

Probably every woman has had some uncomfortable periods—many may have three or four difficult ones a year. But it is not normal to have significant amounts of pain every month.

You are the best barometer of your own feelings, both physical and emotional. If you are in real discomfort before or during your period, and if intercourse is painful for you, you may have endometriosis. If you do or suspect that you do, it's time to get it under treatment and under control.

TWO

CAUSES OF THE CONDITION:
Theories and Myths

THEORIES EXPLAINING ENDOMETRIOSIS

There are a variety of theories about why endometriosis occurs and how it behaves in the body. Most of the theories are inter-related. Currently, most physicians feel that the final answer—and a cure—will rest on a combination of several of these theories.

In this chapter first we'll explore the prevailing theories about the causes of endometriosis; later we'll dispel the many prevailing myths about this mysterious disease.

Retrograde Menstruation

The most widely held theory about how endometriosis develops was suggested by Dr. John Sampson in 1921. His work is still highly thought of, and his is the best explanation offered yet—if only a partial explanation—for this condition. Sampson stated that endometriosis occurs when the lining of the uterus "transplants" itself on other organs of the body.

He noticed that his patients who had the disease did not shed all their menstrual debris with their monthly flow. Instead, it backed up through the fallopian tubes and possibly moved into the pelvic cavity, to the ovaries and elsewhere.

A study conducted in 1984 found that about 90 percent of all women experience some *retrograde menstruation,* as this process is called. But 90 percent of all women don't develop endometriosis, and Sampson's theory fails to account for this.

Autoimmune Deficiency

When we contract a disease, our immune systems protect us by generating fighting cells that resist the invasion of foreign cells. We are able to recover from an illness like the flu, for example, because the body has special flu-fighting cells or *antibodies* that go into action as soon as the flu virus attacks. This virus is marked by its own *antigen,* a kind of flag that the body can recognize. When a particular foreign antigen invades the body, those specially designated antibodies go after it and fight back.

According to the autoimmune-deficiency theory of endometriosis, the typical female reproductive system undergoing retrograde menstruation treats the floating endometrial cells as foreign bodies and rejects them. They gradually become absorbed into the surrounding tissue, causing no changes or disturbances.

But for some unknown reason, this theory holds, certain women have an autoimmune deficiency and don't develop the antibodies that would wipe out these foreign invading cells. Instead of making a brief appearance around the peritoneum and the reproductive organs and then vanishing, the endometrial cells are accepted by the body as host tissue. They implant and begin to grow, most typically on the ovaries and fallopian tubes but sometimes on the bladder, the bowel, and the cul-de-sac (that area behind the uterus).

Increasing numbers of studies show that women with endometriosis may typically suffer from other autoimmune conditions as well. Some of these are rheumatoid arthritis, psoriasis, ulcerative colitis, multiple sclerosis, lupus, and chronic yeast infections (candidiasis).

Increased Prostaglandins

Many of your tissues and organs produce a group of fatty acid derivatives known as *prostaglandins* as part of their immune response. These biological substances have many functions, one of which is to cause the uterus to contract. This contraction creates menstrual cramps. If you have endometriosis, according to this theory, you produce more prostaglandins than women who don't. As your body unsuccessfully tries to fight off the implantation of new endometriosis tissue, your prostaglandins proliferate. The resulting cramps (dysmenorrhea) are typical of endometriosis.

Increased prostaglandins may also affect your ability to conceive. Research has shown that they may be partly responsible for problems with egg-follicle formation and with ovulation.

Transplantation by the Blood and Lymph Systems

This theory tries to explain how the endometrial cells get to their ultimate destination. Either the circulatory system or the lymphatic system or both may pick up bits of the endometrial debris and carry them throughout your body. Since endometrial implants have been found—very rarely—as far away as the lungs, legs, and groin, and occasionally in men who have taken estrogen for prostate conditions, this theory makes a certain amount of sense.

Transplantation by Surgical Procedures (Iatrogenic)

This theory holds that any form of abdominal surgery might help to spread the implants around the pelvic cavity through the bloodstream. Some physicians counsel against performing any exploratory diagnostic procedures during a menstrual period because these procedures produce scar tissue. Endometrial implants are often found in adhesions from previous surgeries.

It is also suspected that various diagnostic procedures in the pelvic cavity—such as a laparoscopy, an endometrial biopsy, or a hysterosalpingogram—might encourage blood and endometrial debris to move throughout the pelvic area and to attach at new sites. (See Chapter 5 for a description of these diagnostic procedures.)

Transformation or Metaplasia— Celomic Theory

Dr. Robert Meyer, a early twentieth-century physician, felt that the endometrial implants looked like the tissue of the endometrium but were not identical to it. He believed that the higher-than-normal levels of estrogen in his patients with endometriosis was responsible for irritating the peritoneum and subsequently causing *metaplasia,* or abnormal cell changes in it.

No firm scientific basis for Meyer's theory has ever been found.

Redwine's Theory

Dr. David Redwine, a gynecologist currently practicing in Bend, Oregon, has developed what he terms a new and innovative approach, although his theory is a direct descendant of Meyer's. Redwine believes that endo is a congenital birth defect. He feels that it is not a progressive disease but a static one that simply changes its appearance over time.

In the female embryo, according to Redwine, endometrial tissue develops from the ducts (Mullerian ducts) that differentiate into ovaries, uterus, and vagina as the fetus grows. Some of the endometrial cells, instead of traveling from the ducts to develop into the uterine lining, stay where they are in the pelvic cavity. In the early preadolescent years, when hormone production starts up, these leftover pieces of tissue start producing the problems of endometriosis.

At birth, Redwine says, the implants are generally clear papules. Over the years, if they are not removed, they darken, first becoming white, then gray-red, yellow, blue, and at last black. Implants that Redwine has seen in autopsies of infant girls indicate to him that the disease has little to do with the hormonal fluctuations of the female reproductive system.

To treat endometriosis, Redwine uses angled scissors and forceps to remove a great deal of the peritoneum—where, in his opinion, most of the implants are located. His method is currently in use by several other physicians around the country. Although statistically the recurrence rate of implants is very low with this type of treatment, it must be noted that the cutting generates scar tissue and adhesions. These adhesions may increase the probability of recurrence of the disease. No studies as yet have evaluated the long-term effects of Redwine's work.

Narrow Cervical Opening

Your cervical opening must be wide enough to permit adequate passage of menstrual debris each month. Some physicians postulate that any type of narrowing of the cervix could prevent adequate passage of menstrual debris.

A variety of congenital defects may contribute to your body's difficulty in ridding itself of endometrial tissue. One such defect is an imperforate hymen that allows no passage of menstrual fluid. Another is the narrowing or actual absence of a cervix. Still another is a vaginal membrane that divides the organ in half. These abnormalities are relatively rare, but they are found in women with endometriosis more frequently than they are found in the general population.

Heredity

A variety of studies have shown that women may have a predisposition to endometriosis if someone in their family had or has the disease. Family members (who are genetically similar) may all have an autoimmune deficiency or increased estrogen levels or some congenital abnormality.

WHAT DO WE KNOW FOR CERTAIN ABOUT ENDOMETRIOSIS?

There are many aspects of endometriosis that medical science still cannot explain. But the most commonly accepted view is that the disease stems from a combination of retrograde menstruation and autoimmune deficiency.

Both past and present experimental research and testing have confirmed the following certainties:

- Endometrial cells can be collected from menstrual flow, which proves that they do travel.

- Endometrial cells can and do implant and grow in the peritoneal cavity.

- It is possible to transplant endo cells collected from the menstrual flow onto the membrane that overlies the abdominal walls.

- Transplanted endometrial cells can start to grow without hormonal stimulation. But they need the estrogen/progesterone cycle in order to thrive. As ovarian hormone levels decrease with age and menopause approaches, endometrial implants tend to shrink and may even vanish.

- The more capillaries and blood vessels in a particular area, the higher the chance that implants will grow there. For example, the pelvic peritoneum is often the site of endometriosis because it's rich with blood sources.

This knowledge about the intricate mechanisms of the disease gives physicians invaluable tools with which to work on your treatment.

MYTHS ABOUT ENDOMETRIOSIS

Because endometriosis still holds so many mysteries, there are a variety of myths about it. These myths must be dispelled if we are to gain any real understanding of the disease.

Myth 1: Endometriosis is primarily a disease of thin, unmarried, Caucasian career-businesswomen.

Although women in any and all of these categories do get endometriosis, the stereotype is far from accurate.

For many years, diagnosis of endometriosis was often made on the basis of a woman's race and economic status. A poor black or ethnic woman who complained of dysmenorrhea, dyspareunia, or infertility would be treated for PID, which is an infection that results from a sexually transmitted disease. But a white middle-class woman who complained of the very same symptoms would be treated for endo. Black women rarely became endo statistics because they weren't affluent enough to make regular gynecological visits and often couldn't afford to pay for the costly hormonal treatments and surgical procedures that endometriosis treatment requires. But race has nothing to do with a woman's predisposition to the disease.

Nor do you have to be thin and athletic to be a candidate for endo. There are heavy-set women who have never jogged or played tennis who suffer badly from the disease. Being *very* athletic can simply mask the symptoms of endo. Athletes in training often stop menstruating—at least, they have lighter periods—because strenuous exercise reduces their estrogen levels. Without the fluctuations of the monthly hormonal cycle, the implants do not bleed and scar. (Smoking cigarettes—at least a pack a day—also lowers the production of estrogen in the body, but no one is recommending that you take up this life-threatening habit in order to take care of your endometriosis.)

The belief that unmarried career women who have never borne children are more likely to have endometriosis is also a myth. A woman who begins childbearing at twenty, has many children, and breastfeeds puts herself in a state of hormonal suspension. She doesn't go through the fluctuations of the monthly cycle for a good many of her reproductive years, so implants are less likely to grow. But having babies doesn't "cure" endo—it simply forestalls the appearance of symptoms.

Who is the most likely candidate for endometriosis? Though the latest research indicates that certain families may have a predisposition to the disease, *any woman* might contract it at any time. You are just as likely to have endometriosis if you are:

- thirteen, have been menstruating for only two years, and have extreme pain before and during menses

- eighteen, have never had sexual intercourse, and have a history of heavy or uncomfortable periods

- twenty-two and unable to conceive or carry a fetus to term

- thirty, have one or two children, and have had no previous history of menstrual problems

- thirty-five and have had no problems whatsoever since you were treated for and supposedly "cured" of endo ten years ago

- Caucasian, black, or Asian; thin or heavy-set; come from any socioeconomic group; a housewife or have a career outside the home.

There is no "typical" endometriosis patient.

Myth 2: Tampon use can cause endo.

Most physicians feel that use of tampons makes no difference in the development of endometriosis. Some doctors even recommend tampons because they believe that they have a drawing effect on the menstrual blood. Other physicians hold the opposite view: they suggest you don't use tampons during heavy-flow days because the absorbent material may tend to trap menstrual debris. They recommend that you wear a pad so that the menstrual debris can simply pass out of the body. You and your physician should discuss this (and all the various issues) together.

Myth 3: Sexual intercourse during your period can cause endometriosis.

Several doctors have posited that the suction caused by the thrusting action of the penis in the vagina may in some way encourage retrograde menstruation. But other physicians believe that orgasm may help prevent retrograde menstruation because the vaginal contractions may help to push menstrual debris out.

Myth 4: An IUD is as safe a birth-control alternative as a diaphragm if you have endometriosis.

Most physicians feel that it is not advisable to use an IUD for birth control if you have endometriosis. One reason for this is that the IUD obstructs the cervix and therefore blocks the passage of menstrual debris. More to the point, the volume of menstrual blood increases by 50 to 100 percent after the insertion of either an inert or a copper-based IUD. The more menstrual blood produced each month, the more likely that debris will reflux back into the pelvic cavity.

A diaphragm, on the other hand, is recommended for several reasons. As a barrier contraceptive, it forms a protective shield against sexually transmitted diseases. Because it is removed and cleaned hours after use, cervical and vaginal secretions (and menstrual debris, if it's used during your period) are not able to pool in the vaginal canal or reflux back into the pelvic cavity.

Myth 5: The only sure cure for endometriosis is a hysterectomy.

A hysterectomy is a possible cure for endometriosis, but it is not a sure cure. It has given thousands of women who no longer want or hope for children relief from chronic pain and lifted restrictions on their activity. But most physicians currently feel that a hysterectomy (removal of the uterus alone) is not sufficient for a woman with chronic endometriosis. Instead, they recommend definitive surgery in which the ovaries and tubes are also removed. This is called a "clean-out" or a *total abdominal hysterectomy and bilateral salpingo-oophorectomy (TAHBSO).*

If the estrogen- and progesterone-producing organs are gone, the most prevalent areas for endometrial implants are removed from the picture and there is no hormonal stimulation to keep the implants going (see Chapter 8).

But a few women still suffer great pain from endometriosis after the removal of their reproductive organs. Implants may have become attached to a nonreproductive organ, such as the bladder or bowel, or even in the hip or lungs. Although these implants no longer receive hormonal stimulation because the woman no longer has ovaries to generate estrogen and progesterone, many other factors in the endometriosis picture (prostaglandins and the proximity of implants to nerve endings, among others) may contribute to the continuation of their symptoms. If you are experiencing such pain, your physician may recommend a course of medication to shrink the remaining implants.

Myth 6: Stress causes endometriosis.

Being in debilitating pain does put you under enormous stress. Moreover, if sexual intimacy is uncomfortable or impossible, that will create a lot of tension and stress in your marriage too. And certainly, the procedures and delays involved in an infertility workup are enormously stressful. Finally, it has been postulated that being under stress lowers your immune resistance— it's easier to pick up viruses and flus when you're stressed out. But there is absolutely no evidence that stress *causes* endometriosis.

SORTING FACT FROM FICTION

No one knows exactly what causes endometriosis or why some women develop it and others don't. If you have been diagnosed with endometriosis, you may be concerned and confused because your doctor can give you no definite explanation of why you developed the disease.

The research of the next decade may well produce a better picture of how all the facets involved in endometriosis fit together. Until science puts all the pieces of the puzzle in place, however, your doctor is limited to working with the various surgical and hormonal regimens at his or her disposal.

You can't begin to seek relief from your symptoms until you have definitive proof that you have the disease. The next chapter deals with the crucial teamwork of doctor and patient as together they search for a correct diagnosis.

THREE

DIAGNOSIS:
The Joint Task of
Doctor and Patient

Although endometriosis is exceptionally difficult to diagnose, with proper medical care you can get into treatment promptly. It is important to be under the care of a physician you trust who is familiar with the variable nature of the disease. Because endometriosis is a chronic condition—that is, one that continues for years—it is doubly crucial that your relationship with your primary caregiver be satisfying and productive for both of you.

Losing time at work is one of the biggest cost factors in endometriosis. If you're in chronic pain, you may spend two or more days a month in bed. This can have a profound effect on your relationship with your employer, and it can severely damage your own sense of worth about handling responsibility. The longer you go without a correct diagnosis, without being on a course of treatment that works for you, the more your life will be disrupted. This is yet another reason why finding an understanding, expert physician familiar with the disease is an absolute necessity. This chapter will help you in your search for the right practitioner and the right treatment.

If you are currently under the care of a physician who appears to be confused about your symptoms or impatient with your questions, or who provides you with treatment that is not giving you relief, it is time for you to think about changing doctors.

Many women with endometriosis ride a disturbing merry-go-round of medical care, jumping off one horse and climbing onto the next for as many as ten or fifteen years, without actually learning what is wrong with them.

This unsettling pattern—with its attendant pain, anger, and general mistrust of the medical profession—can affect your life deeply. Never to know whether you can go through your daily activities, have a family, or enjoy physical activity is a terrible bind in which to put yourself.

But you can break that pattern by learning everything you can about the disease and putting this new knowledge into action. The amount of information about endometriosis now in the public domain makes it unnecessary—as well as unproductive—for you to stay uninformed. You don't have to feel sorry for yourself and angry at others. Hope and help are available, but it's up to you to find them.

In order to get properly diagnosed and into appropriate treatment, you must take the upper hand in selecting a physician. Once you've found him or her, you have an obligation to become partners in managing your disease so that together you can make important decisions and conduct a treatment program that is workable for both of you.

INFORMING YOURSELF

You are not a doctor; therefore, you are not expected to know particulars about the stages of the disease, the different drugs available and their dosages, or different surgical options and techniques. But you should be able to describe your medical history and your symptoms and keep accurate records of the various cycles of your condition. You should be able to ask your doctor intelligent questions based on your knowledge, and you should be able to answer his or her questions about your menstrual cycle, your pain, your bleeding, your activity level, your sexual history, and the like.

If you believe you have endometriosis, use the resources around you to find out as much as you can about the disease. Your public library and the Endometriosis Association (see Chapter 11) are your first and best sources of information. Do some reading, compare your symptoms and patterns to the descriptions in this book, and go to your next doctor's appointment armed with questions. In the process you may be surprised to find that you are educating your physician, particularly if he or she is a family doctor or an obstetrics-gynecology practitioner. If he or she can't answer your questions, this may be an indication that you should see a specialist.

FINDING AN APPROPRIATE PHYSICIAN

When you have educated yourself enough to have an intelligent discussion with your doctor based on your knowledge, you've taken an important step toward getting diagnosed. Ask your questions in a probing manner, without appearing aggressive or hostile. Your goal is to find out whether you should continue paying this professional for his or her services, or if you should seek help elsewhere.

If you've been seeing the same family physician or obstetrician/gynecologist for years without relief from your symptoms, you should either change your relationship with this doctor or find a new health-care practitioner.

If you do decide to get another opinion, ask your nearest

university **hospital or** your state medical board to give you a list of qualified **practitioners** who are board certified in reproductive endocrinology or fertility. If you are troubled by the thought of making a selection on your own, the Endometriosis Association (see Chapter 11) can provide you with a contact list of endometriosis patients and chapters in your area. There are support groups all over the United States, Canada, and Europe. The women you will meet in these groups can give you names of sympathetic physicians who are familiar with the treatment of endo.

You will undoubtedly come across someone who feels her doctor:

- is a good listener and a good talker

- takes her problems seriously

- is able to describe procedures in nonthreatening ways, in layman's terms

- is patient and compassionate

- is up on the latest information in the field

- is willing to admit that he or she doesn't know all the answers

You may find that when you call the best person with the best referrals in your area, you are told by the nurse or secretary that it will be two months before you can have an appointment. Don't give up hope—the very good people in the field are very busy.

YOUR EXPECTATIONS
ABOUT YOUR DOCTOR

You may have your own criteria for choosing a doctor. For example, you may feel more comfortable with a physician of one sex or another. Or you may want your doctor to be affiliated with a certain hospital of high repute. You probably want a doctor who is accessible by public transportation or within no more than an hour's drive from your home or office.

Some endometriosis experts around the country offer specialized care to those who travel to their office or clinic for treatment. Although their credentials may be impressive, it is not a good idea to select a physician located far from your home. The best doctor-patient relationship for this condition is one that is forged over many years and that relies on weekly or sometimes daily phone contact.

Although high-tech medicine has developed far beyond the comprehension of most lay people, this does not mean that you should accept a treatment that you don't understand and whose benefits and drawbacks are unclear to you. Because decisions made about the treatment of endometriosis often affect life decisions, such as marriage, career and family, it is crucial that you have a say in the how, when, why, and where of your treatment.

WHAT YOUR DOCTOR WANTS YOU
TO TELL HIM OR HER

A new physician with whom you have just begun a relationship will want to see your medical records from your previous doctor or doctors. These are yours for the asking, and your previous doctor will forward them to your new doctor as soon as you write and request them. You may want to make a follow-up telephone call to make sure your records have been sent promptly.

Your first interview and examination should take place on the day before or during your period, when your implants are most likely to be engorged with blood and therefore easier to detect. When you make your appointment, tell the secretary or nurse on the phone when you expect your next cycle to begin.

Your initial consultation and exam will probably last an hour, sometimes two. Endometriosis patients fall into two categories —those dealing with pain, and those who wish to become pregnant. So the doctor will first want to know which category you are in.

The doctor will then take a thorough *medical history.* When he or she asks you about your symptoms, you may find it helpful to refer to notes. So if you have not done so, you should begin to keep an *endometriosis diary.* In this diary you should indicate the dates of your periods, their severity, any unusual characteristics (such as passing blood clots or spotting in between periods). You should note whether you had pain, when it began and ended in relation to your cycle, and whether it was worse or better than last month. Bring this diary with you to every exam.

The doctor will ask you what year your periods began, whether they were regular, how many days you typically bled, whether you experienced premenstrual pain and cramping, and whether you took medication to alleviate the pain—Motrin, Tylenol, or a prescription pain-killer like codeine. He'll ask whether the pain has gotten worse or remained the same over time.

You should be able to *describe the pain* in words and gestures. (Many women make a fist and twist it inward toward their groin area to show the gut-wrenching aspect of endo pain.)

The doctor will want to know what *other symptoms* you have, if any.

- Do you have bleeding or spotting in between periods?

- Is it difficult for you to urinate or defecate during periods, and is there any bleeding?

- Do you have abdominal tenderness or bloating?

- Do you ever have gastrointestinal or flulike symptoms around the time of your period? Are you ever constipated? Do you have diarrhea?

- Do you ever experience dizziness, headaches, fever, chronic fatigue, or lower back pain?

- Do your symptoms keep you from performing your daily activities?

If you are seeing the doctor because you've been unable to conceive or have had repeated miscarriages, the doctor will concentrate most of the questioning on *infertility* (see Chapter 7).

The doctor will ask whether anyone else in your *family* has been diagnosed with endometriosis or has had difficulties with menstrual pain or with infertility. (If anyone has, your doctor might want to speak with her physician.)

The doctor will ask you questions about your *sexual life:* When did you become sexually active? Did you find intercourse uncomfortable? Were any positions better than others? What kind of contraceptive do you use? If you have ever been on birth control pills, did you notice that your periods were any easier?

THE DIAGNOSIS

After a lengthy discussion, the physician will ask you to put on a robe and go into the examining room. You'll be asked to leave a urine sample, and the doctor will take a blood sample. The doctor will want to test your hormonal levels since very often, women with endo have elevated estrogens. (There is currently no blood test to detect endometriosis, but there is a component of blood known as CA-125 that is typically elevated in women with endometriosis. Unfortunately, it can be elevated for other reasons, too, and the test is not sensitive enough to use for a general indicator. It may be helpful, however, in monitoring the disease once a definite diagnosis is made.)

The physician will do a routine breast and abdominal check, then an internal. He or she will insert a speculum to look at your cervix and will take a Pap smear. Then he or she will do a *bimanual exam,* inserting a finger of one hand into your vagina and sweeping the internal organs—the uterus, tubes, and ovaries—with the other, from the outside. (This exam can be painful if you have endometriosis implants anywhere in the area the physician is manipulating.) He or she will then do a *rectal exam* to feel behind the uterus.

Women with endometriosis of the cul-de-sac (the area right behind the uterus) commonly have the problem that their uterus has little range of flexibility. In fact, it may be "frozen" if the adhesions have bound the usually flexible organ into one place. If this has happened, the slightest attempt to manipulate it may cause excruciating pain.

Another strong indication that you may have endometriosis is if the doctor feels nodules—sometimes known as "rosary beads"—on the uterosacral ligaments, which connect the pelvis with the spinal column. He or she may also feel a mass or a cyst somewhere in the pelvic cavity—most typically on an ovary.

TESTS CAN GIVE AN INDICATION
OF ENDOMETRIOSIS

If your physician feels a mass in your pelvis, he or she will probably want to do an *ultrasound*. Many doctors have the equipment for this in their offices; others will have to send you to the hospital to have the test.

Ultrasound is a completely painless test in which sound waves are bounced off soft tissue to detect the existence and location of cysts or tumors in the body. Some studies on pregnant women have found that ultrasound may produce certain slight internal changes. To date, the test has not been definitively proven to cause any harm—unlike X rays, which use radiation to examine hard tissue (bone and cartilage). The doctor cannot be certain what kind of mass you have based on the results of the ultrasound alone.

If you have been having severe gastrointestinal symptoms— particularly if you've noticed blood in your stool around the time of your period—the doctor may order a *barium enema*. This test is not pleasant, but it should not be painful either. The bowel must be cleaned out beforehand; to do this, you must follow a specific diet for several days before the procedure, then undergo repeated enemas. You'll probably be sent to a radiology lab to have the test. There, barium sulfate will be inserted into your colon through a tube up the rectum. This will facilitate X-ray and fluoroscopic examination of the colon. Air may also be inserted to provide contrast with the barium in the photograph. If you have endometrial implants in the bowel or colon, they may show up clearly on the X ray.

If you see blood in your urine or have a constant need to urinate, you may have endometriosis in your bladder or kidney area. A test called an *intravenous pyelogram* (IVP) can be done, in which dye is injected into a vein and travels to the kidneys so that they can be visualized on an X ray. A *cystoscopy* is another test for this purpose—a thin tube with a built-in light source is inserted into the urethra. A biopsy of the urinary tract can be taken with this instrument to examine tissue that might have endometrial implants.

If these tests and the examination show evidence of endometriosis, your doctor will carefully explain his or her findings and suspicions to you. *Remember that your doctor cannot tell you anything for certain or begin treatment at this point. The only way he or she can make a definite diagnosis of endometriosis is to perform a laparoscopy, a surgical procedure usually performed under anesthesia in a hospital.* (see Chapter 5).

FOLLOW-UP AFTER SURGICAL DIAGNOSIS

If your doctor finds any tissue that may be endometrial during the laparoscopy, he or she will send it to the laboratory to be biopsied. This will show for certain whether you have endometriosis. From looking inside, the doctor will know whether you have a mild or minimal form of the disease (Stage I or Stage II) or a moderate or severe form (Stage III or Stage IV).

By the time you wake up from the anesthesia, your doctor will have a better idea of the extent of your disease and what your treatment options are. He or she might suggest hormonal suppression, surgery, or a combination of both. The doctor will go over his findings with you in the hospital and at your next office visit, which will probably be sometime in the next few days.

At this point, the two of you will discuss all the options available. If you're trying to get pregnant, the doctor probably won't have you do anything more except try to conceive. Pregnancy has long been touted as a temporary stopgap for endometriosis because it stops your monthly cycling. The absence of periods for nine months and perhaps for three more after the birth (longer if you breastfeed) gives the implants no occasion to swell, bleed, and scar over. In some cases, however, pregnancy makes endometriosis symptoms even worse. Since there are so many complicating factors other than hormonal fluctuation involved in the disease, pregnancy may not change your medical picture at all. On the other hand, there have also been cases where pregnancy caused temporary or permanent remission of the disease.

If childbearing is not an issue but relief from pain and other symptoms is, your doctor will undoubtedly put you on one of the several available forms of hormonal suppression (see Chapter 6). He or she will discuss the various pros, cons, and side effects of these medications. If the laparoscopy has indicated that your disease is extensive, he or she may suggest laser laparoscopy to remove the visible implants and lesions.

If you have a large cyst or complex adhesions, your doctor may feel that a *laparotomy,* or open surgery, will allow him or her to remove all visible evidence of endometriosis (see Chapter 8).

If your disease is severe, if you have tried every other appropriate method of treatment, and if you have no further desire to conceive, your doctor may suggest radical or definitive surgery (see Chapter 8). If so, he or she will indicate when that surgery should be performed and whether you should be on a course of medication before and/or after it.

COSTS OF TREATMENT

It's very important to be up front about asking what the various treatments cost and how the doctor expects to be paid. You should be familiar with your own insurance situation. If you don't know what kind of coverage your policy has, find out at once.

Endometriosis can be an expensive disease. Though more and more insurance companies cover up to 100 percent of the surgical and drug treatments, office visits, and hospitalization, some do not. Remember that you will have to pay the first amounts incurred up to your deductible; some physicians require that you pay them and have your insurance company reimburse you afterward.

AVOID FRUSTRATION—
BE HONEST WITH EACH OTHER

Throughout the diagnostic procedure, it's crucial that you be extremely open and honest with your doctor and that he or she extend you the same courtesy. The only way you're going to work together is through communication.

Ask your doctor the following questions:

- How long do the different forms of treatment take?

- What are the expected results of the various treatments?

- Will there be a recovery period after surgery?

- Will I have to miss any work or school?

- How often will I have office appointments?

- What are the best times of day to call you?

- What are the side effects of the drugs you're prescribing?

- How often do you do this kind of surgery?

The physician will have diplomas and certificates on his wall, but it's useful to ask directly, *particularly* about special training in laser surgery.

Be thorough and discuss every issue:

- whether you're afraid of hospitals and surgery

- whether your spouse, a friend, or a relative can be with you

- how the various treatments affect your decision about childbearing and your fertility

- what the doctor's success rate is with patients with endometriosis

Ask the doctor for an honest appraisal of your condition. A good doctor will give you an optimistic but realistic response, neither a promise of a cure nor a dire warning that your treatment will be long and difficult. If your doctor makes claims of miraculous results from any innovative surgical techniques, it's a good idea to check into them. The choice of treatment is always up to you, and when it comes to radical or definitive surgery, you should get a second opinion before committing yourself. (Most insurance companies insist on it.)

You have every right to expect your doctor to make a conscientious effort not only to inform you but to be there for you, not as a pal but as a concerned professional. He or she should keep you abreast of changes in your condition and of new developments in the field as they occur—and explain them so that you can understand.

Help yourself by taking notes every time you talk to your doctor. Emotionally loaded information is often difficult to remember, and for this reason, a small tape recorder or a notepad and pen are absolutely essential during every consultation, both on the phone and in person.

After the doctor has told you something, repeat it back to him or her in your own words, to be certain you've understood.

Remember that *every* patient is different. Some women are desperate for pain relief and have no concern about whether they can get pregnant within a year. Others are self-conscious and anxious about the possible side effects of drugs. Some patients want reassurance and support from their doctors on a weekly—even a daily—basis by phone. Others prefer to see their physicians only for necessary appointments.

Decide what you want out of the doctor-patient relationship, and take charge of your selection so that you can get just what you feel you need. As a patient and a medical consumer, you have every right to have your condition diagnosed and treated in a manner acceptable to you.

FOUR

WHAT KIND OF ENDO DO YOU HAVE?
A Classification

Endometriosis is classified according to four stages—ranging from "minimal, Stage I" to "severe, Stage IV"—for greater ease of diagnosis. Only when you and your physician reach an understanding of what kind of endometriosis you have will deciding on an appropriate treatment be possible.

You may walk into your doctor's office in a great deal of pain, and after the examination the doctor may tell you that you have "minimal to mild" endometriosis. He or she is *not* in any way making light of your condition but is only referring to the American Fertility Society (AFS) classification system. This classification system was devised primarily to deduce a woman's chances of conceiving, but it also happens to offer a good handle for doctors and patients in dealing with the difficult, changeable disease of endometriosis.

THE AMERICAN FERTILITY
SOCIETY CLASSIFICATION

The AFS classification system, which the society updated most recently in 1985, uses a numbered point scale to give values to the number, size, and location of the various implants, cysts, or lesions a woman has at a particular time. It gives your doctor a way to rate your level of disease and a way to talk to other doctors about your disease in concrete terms.

The greatest flaw of this system is that it describes only what the doctor can see in your pelvis on surgical examination. There is no method for labeling the changes that might be going on in your immune system or the various elements in your blood that might contribute to the disease. Nor is any allowance made for the fact that most implants fluctuate in size over the course of a month, according to the hormonal influence they're under.

There are four stages of endometriosis in the system. Each particular case is specifically assigned a number of points. There are seven location sites on the classification chart: ovaries, fallopian tubes, bladder, bowel, appendix, peritoneum, and cul-de-sac.

- Stage I (minimal); Only the peritoneum and right ovary are involved, and the adhesions or implants are superficial (1 to 5 points).

- Stage II (mild); The peritoneum and both ovaries are involved, and the implants may be superficial or deep (6 to 15 points).

- Stage III (moderate); The peritoneum, cul-de-sac, both tubes, and both ovaries may be involved (16 to 40 points).

- Stage IV (severe); There is considerable disease in many or all of the seven possible locations (more than 40 points).

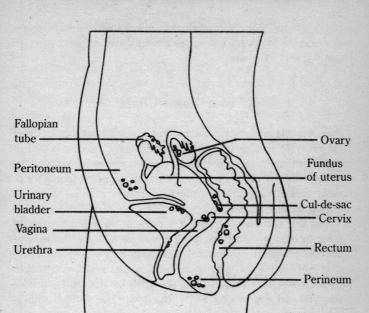

Figure 2 Common sites of endometriosis
(clockwise from top right: ovary, fundus of uterus, cul-de-sac,
cervix, rectum, perineum, urethra, vagina, urinary bladder,
peritoneum, fallopian tube)

Endometriosis appears in different manifestations in various
patients and is described in many ways, but the classification
system zeroes in on certain words that all doctors use in their
descriptions.

Implants are either *filmy* or *dense;* they are also either *superficial* or *deep.* In the minimal to mild forms of the disease, the

physician may see only superficial implants on the peritoneum; in moderate to severe cases, the growths may go down through many layers of tissue.

Your Point Chart

After your laparoscopy, your physician will fill out a point chart for you. He or she will update it whenever necessary—after treatment and/or a second-look laparoscopy; every six months at your regular exam, or sooner if you're under hormonal treatment and coming in on a more frequent basis; or if you're having further surgery.

You can and should request a copy of your point chart to refer to or, if you have decided to change doctors, to show to another physician at an initial consultation.

If you are currently in some form of treatment, you should check to see that your chart is the 1985 version, to be certain that you and your doctor are working with the same classification system.

Endometriosis in Nonreproductive Organs

The classification chart does not account for endometriosis that occurs in the cervix, vagina, vulva, intestinal tract, urinary tract, abdominal wall, thoracic cage and lungs, arms, legs or central nervous system. Endometriosis has been found in every part of the body except the spleen, which for some unexplained reason seems to suppress the growth of these implants or lesions. The American Fertility Society chose not to include these extrapelvic locations in its chart because the incidence there is much lower than in the seven pelvic areas.

Most extrapelvic endo is treated with hormones first and, if that is unsuccessful, with surgery. In extreme cases—for example, if the ureter is blocked and the patient risks losing kidney function—radical surgery may be necessary.

The Differences between the Stages of Endometriosis

The AFS classification system is intended only to indicate a woman's chances of conception. The point system and the involvement of different organs at different levels are significant for fertility, not for pain. Even microscopic implants can cause agonizing, excruciating pain, whereas an endometrioma the size of an orange may not even be noticed by the patient.

WHAT DOES ENDOMETRIOSIS LOOK LIKE?

Some physicians are beginning to believe that endometriosis is actually many diseases. This is because it can look very different in many patients in many locations. Implants can be filmy or dense; in addition, they can be many different colors; they can be microscopic or as big as a grapefruit; they can look a certain way at an initial laparoscopy, and look totally different six months later during a second-look laparoscopy.

Forms

Endometriosis appears in many forms. The displaced tissue may develop into nodules, tumors, lesions, implants, growths,

or adhesions. Any or all of these can cause pain and infertility—
or no symptoms at all.

An *endometrioma* is a cyst that typically attaches itself to one
of the ovaries. It is often called a chocolate cyst because it is
filled with dark, old blood from repeated cycles of bleeding and
scarring over. During a course of hormonal suppression, these
cysts may lose their firm, velvet texture and become soft and
gelatinous, putting them at risk of rupturing internally. For this
reason many physicians avoid prescribing hormones to women
with endometriomas.

Your doctor can feel a mass during the bimanual exam but
will not know immediately if it is an endometrioma. It could be
one of many things—a benign fibroid, a malignant ovarian tumor, an ectopic pregnancy. An ultrasound will give your doctor
the exact location and size of the mass, but only a laparoscopy
and a tissue biopsy will tell for sure whether it is an endometrioma or something else.

Colors

Some small endometrial implants often look like black pinhead-
size blemishes, called *black powder-burn* implants. There may
be only a few such lesions, or an area may be covered with
them as if it had been sprayed with gunpowder.

Other lesions look whitish in color, almost like whiteheads
on the face. Still others are clear, yellow, gray, blue, and red.
Physicians have described implants as mulberry, raspberry, or
blueberry spots. The particular color of each lesion is located in
the *glands* of the endometriosis cells; the bed or foundation
around them, known as the *stroma,* is the part that bleeds.

It requires a sharp eye to distinguish some of these implants
and eradicate them all with the laser or scalpel. Even if your
doctor is reasonably sure that he or she has gotten everything,

your condition may still recur. Over a six-month period microscopic implants may grow and become visible, or new implants may appear.

FERTILITY AND THE POINT SCALE

Your prospects of conceiving and carrying a fetus to term are much better if your endometriosis is mild or minimal, no matter how terrible your pain is. Your fertility may have less to do with your endometriosis than with the routine functioning of your endocrine system. It has been proven that women with endometriosis typically have more problems with the second half of their hormonal cycle, the luteal phase (which occurs after ovulation), than women without endo (see Chapter 7).

Moderate to severe endometriosis presents a much more difficult arena for conception and for maintaining a pregnancy. If the thick adhesions and overgrowth of tissue have bound the organs in place and if the ovary and tubes are twisted out of alignment, normal passage of an egg from the ovary through the tubes and into the uterus is impossible (see Chapter 7).

THE GROWTH RATE OF ENDOMETRIOSIS

Although most physicians feel that endometriosis is a progressive condition, it may be halted at a particular stage or it may even go into remission. If it gets worse, it usually does so very slowly, which allows you and your doctor time to take the right steps toward prudent management.

Most doctors consider Stages III and IV a very different disease from Stages I and II. The high point-ratings of the Stage III and IV disease require much more management and much more surgery, and the infertility problems are far more difficult.

If you are initially diagnosed as having minimal to mild endometriosis, *you will probably remain in the Stage I or Stage II category throughout your life.* Although the location and severity of your disease may fluctuate slightly, it is highly unlikely that you will jump from Stage I to Stage III or Stage IV.

But even if you feel fine during the time that you're off medication, you must be certain to have regular checkups. In some cases people have jumped a stage or two because they had no symptoms and were not under a doctor's care—and therefore they were not aware of the slow and insidious growth of their disease. It is entirely possible to have only minimal black powder-burn implants at your initial laparoscopy, go through a six-month course of birth-control pills and feel fine, then discover after a second-look laparoscopy that you've developed a three-millimeter cyst on your ovary.

Because the disease is so unpredictable, you must stay in close touch with your physician. He or she will probably want to see you every six months, regardless of how you feel, and maybe more frequently if you're on a course of hormones. If your old symptoms are recurring or if new ones are developing that you suspect may be connected with your endometriosis, call your physician immediately.

LAPAROSCOPY:
The Major Tool for Diagnosis and Treatment

The only way to get a definitive diagnosis of endometriosis is by the surgical procedure known as a *laparoscopy*. The doctor must see the inside of your pelvic cavity in order to determine whether you have endometriosis and how best to treat it.

In diagnosing most chronic medical conditions, we tend to think of surgery as a last resort, after all the blood tests and X rays and sonograms and CT scans have failed to offer conclusive proof. But a surgical investigation and a biopsy of the suspected tissue is the *only* way to prove that you have endometriosis.

There is currently no blood test that can detect the condition, and though a sonogram will pick up a soft mass like a cyst, it cannot produce a picture of the tiny black-powder-burn evidence of endometriosis. Nor would your physician feel comfortable starting you on a course of medication without being absolutely certain that you have endometriosis. This is why he will recommend a laparoscopy if he or she suspects that you have endo.

WHY IS A LAPAROSCOPY ESSENTIAL IN ENDOMETRIOSIS TREATMENT?

A laparoscopy is not major open surgery. The surgeon makes only an inch-long incision under the belly button and inserts a sort of telescope. Through this, he or she scans your internal organs to look for visible evidence of the disease. Laparoscopy can't be considered a minor surgical procedure because it is invasive and requires general anesthesia. But it is the only definitive diagnostic tool for this disease.

Having a laparoscopy when you first start having symptoms in the minimal or mild stage can mean early detection of your disease. If you have visible implants and lesions, your doctor can use laparoscopy not just for diagnosis but for treatment as well. Removing the endometrial implants during either the initial or the second-look laparoscopy can postpone or eliminate the need for radical or definitive surgery later on (see Chapter 8).

A laparoscopy will tell you not only that you *do* have endometriosis but that you *don't* have some other disease, such as ovarian cancer or an ectopic pregnancy. If you are experiencing pain because of an infection, the physician will be able to determine which bacteria have caused it by taking a culture from the site. Or if your pain is caused by an IUD that has perforated your uterus, the surgeon can remove the IUD with forceps inserted through the laparoscope.

WHEN IS A LAPAROSCOPY UNNECESSARY?

If you are not in chronic pain and your major interest is in getting pregnant, your physician may advise that you wait before having a laparoscopy. Even if your pelvic exam has indicated that some minimal to mild disease may be present (that is, some tenderness or rosary bead nodules on your ligaments), it's more important to concentrate on your first medical priority. Your doctor will probably encourage you to attempt to conceive and ask to see you in another six months, or sooner if you begin to experience any pain. In today's world of astronomical medical costs and uncertain insurance coverage, the wisest medical course is to avoid expensive surgical procedures until they become necessary.

LAPAROSCOPY FOR DIAGNOSIS AND TREATMENT

If you agree to the laparoscopy, you will be admitted to the hospital for an overnight stay. You and your doctor will decide beforehand whether you want him to use the laparoscopy *only* for diagnosis or to remove any visible implants and cysts he finds while you are on the operating table. If you agree to the latter, you will sign a consent form to that effect before your surgery.

Some physicians feel that you should agree to surgical treatment even before *you* know the extent of your disease. In other words, they feel you should allow them to laser or cut out any lesions or implants they see during the initial laparoscopy. The reason is that this saves you both time and money. One procedure means one surgical fee, one time in the operating room, only one night of a hospital stay, and one period of recuperation instead of two. Moreover, if your doctor uses the laser on your implants the first time, your endometriosis has less opportunity to worsen in the intervening weeks before a second surgery is scheduled.

On the other hand, some physicians are opposed to performing a surgical procedure when they have you on the table only for a diagnosis. If you have only a few powder-burn lesions, many doctors feel that your disease can be managed very well with a course of birth control pills (see Chapter 6). You might not need the extra expense and extra risk of a second operation to have your implants lasered or cut away. Discuss your own particular situation carefully with your physician before you decide on the best course of action, and when to take it. *Your goal is a form of treatment that's low in risk and high in efficacy.*

Some physicians perform diagnostic laparoscopies in their offices or in clinics on an out-patient basis. But because general anesthesia is recommended, most doctors do the procedure in a hospital, and an overnight stay is required.

THE COST OF A LAPAROSCOPY

A diagnostic laparoscopy costs anywhere from about $1,000 to $1,500, depending on what state you live in. A laser laparoscopy for treatment starts at $2,500 and goes up depending on the extent of the disease and subsequent operating-room time needed. Many insurance companies will pay 100 percent of the costs, but it's vital that you check with your company ahead of time.

WHAT HAPPENS BEFORE
A LAPAROSCOPY

Before your laparoscopy, you will be asked to fast for twelve hours and to drink only water after dinner the night before. Your doctor will probably order a mini–bowel preparation for you the evening before your surgery. This involves drinking a bottle of citrate of magnesia and giving yourself a Fleet enema to clean out your bowel. If the bowel is full, it's harder for the surgeon to move it around, which he or she must do in order to get a good look in every area of the pelvis. Also, implants and lesions often grow on the bowel or rectum, and if your doctor is using a laser, cautery, or scalpel on your colon or bowel, he or she certainly doesn't want any bacteria that might be present in stool to leach out into the pelvis.

You will be mildly sedated before you are taken up to the operating room.

WHAT HAPPENS DURING A LAPAROSCOPY

You will be anesthetized on the operating table. The doctor will make a small incision beneath your belly button and insert carbon dioxide gas through a needle to inflate the abdomen and separate the pelvic organs for a better view. He or she will then withdraw the needle and put in the laparoscope—a tube about eighteen inches long with a sort of telescope at the end and a sleeve around it that supplies a continual flow of the gas.

A blunt instrument called a *cannula* will be inserted up your vagina through the cervix to facilitate movement of the uterus so that the doctor can see around it.

When the surgeon looks through the laparoscope, he or she will be able to get a panoramic look at your pelvic cavity and see the location, size, and color of any cysts or implants. He can focus in to within a centimeter of the peritoneum and see the implants magnified about six times. He will note whether the disease is mild or severe, whether there are big masses or cysts or weblike adhesions, and whether they have obstructed organs, glued them together, or twisted them out of shape so that they are dysfunctional.

The surgeon will take a *biopsy*, or a small piece of tissue, from any area where disease seems to be present. This tissue will be examined in the pathology laboratory, and findings of the existence or absence of endometriosis will be the concluding piece of evidence in the doctor's diagnosis.

When you wake up from the general anesthesia, you will have only a Band-Aid over your incisions. You will feel moderate to severe aching in your shoulders and upper arms, caused by the accumulation of carbon dioxide when you were tilted backward on the operating table.

VIDEOLAPAROSCOPY

Some physicians use a *videolaparoscope,* which is a laparoscope fitted with a tiny video camera. Its view of the inside of the pelvic cavity is projected onto a TV screen above the doctor, which allows him or her to work comfortably, standing up, instead of bent over the operating table. Another advantage of the video is that it makes a permanent record of the operation. This is useful for monitoring the progress of your disease. And if you should decide to change doctors, the videotape will be part of your medical record. It will give your new physician an invaluable set of findings with which to start treatment.

IMPLANT REMOVAL
DURING LAPAROSCOPY

If you and your physician have so agreed beforehand, he or she will plan to remove your implants surgically during your laparoscopy. If you are going to have laparoscopic surgery, two or possibly three tiny incisions or punctures will be made about four inches below the belly-button incision on either side of the pubic hairline. A suction device will be inserted through one of these openings to remove excess blood and any cellular debris that might collect. The puncture holes also allow the escape of smoke—a natural byproduct of vaporizing or burning tissue with the laser or cautery.

Your doctor will be able to operate only on those lesions or cysts that are small enough to be removed through the incision. Most surgeons draw the line at an endometrioma of three or four millimeters, and reserve anything larger for subsequent open surgery, which is known as a *laparotomy* (see Chapter 8).

The physician will remove as much as possible either by cutting (blunt or sharp), burning (cautery), or vaporizing (turning into water) with a light beam, or laser. He may use all three surgical methods, depending on the type and location of your endometriosis.

Excision

Excision involves the use of scalpel or scissors to scrape and cut away diseased tissue, such as cysts, from organs and tissue. Areas of the peritoneum surrounding small implants can be removed by snipping; then a forceps is used to spread and scrape healthy tissue away from endometrial tissue. Although all surgeons are trained in use of the scalpel and scissors and therefore have the most practice in use of this surgical method, excision does have certain drawbacks. Cutting causes bleeding and requires suturing. As sutures heal, they form scar tissue, which may encourage the regrowth of endometriosis adhesions.

Cautery

Cautery uses an electrical current to burn off the implants or lesions. The problem with cautery is that it is not as precise as the laser and can burn healthy tissue around the endometrial site as well. It is also difficult to control the depth of the burn. In a delicate area, such as the bowel, bladder, or ureter, cautery may be risky. Some surgeons use electrocautery to stop bleeding at a site they have lasered or cut.

Laser

Laser is rapidly becoming the most popular method of surgical treatment for endometriosis because *it is safe and accurate in the hands of a well-trained surgeon.*

Laser, an acronym for "light amplification by stimulated emission of radiation," converts electrical energy to light energy in order to vaporize tissue. The laser beam concentrates a certain frequency of light down to a pinpoint and destroys diseased tissue without touching the healthy tissue around it. The beam heats up to about 2,000 degrees Fahrenheit and energizes the cells to such an extent that they burst open, leaving a tiny hole. The surgeon then suctions away the cellular debris that has been released. A laser can coagulate the blood vessels it shines on. It can vaporize an implant, turning it to steam, then water.

Laser surgery involves very little bleeding—and therefore results in less suturing and subsequent development of scar tissue. When there's less bleeding, the surgeon can see his field better and be more certain of getting all the implants.

Three types of lasers are currently in use:

The *CO_2 laser* uses an infrared beam to vaporize cells. The CO_2 laser is good for surface destruction because the beam is straight and can be shined back and forth over an area, destroying only the first few cells it touches. With the CO_2, what you see is what you get. But because the beam doesn't bend, it can't be used to attack implants that may be behind other organs or at a deeper layer. And because the beam doesn't transmit through blood or fluid, there is a certain amount of bleeding. Electrocautery is generally used in conjunction with the CO_2 laser to cauterize blood vessels.

The *Yttrium Aluminum Garnet (Nd: YAG) laser* is an extremely powerful instrument, created to control bleeding ulcers. It will penetrate three to five millimeters into tissue, which means that it must be handled by a very skillful surgeon —particularly in delicate areas like the ureter and the bowel.

The *KTP laser* is an excellent instrument for operating on endometrial implants. It's a fiber-optic laser and therefore can bend around and under organs. It's not as powerful as the YAG, so it's safer. It can be used to penetrate a little below the surface, yet not so deep that it will destroy underlying tissue. The lesions can be coagulated or vaporized by the range of this green-light laser.

The *Argon laser* is similar to the KTP laser. Though it was originally developed for eye surgeons doing retinal surgery, it's been adapted for gynecological use.

Ask About Your Doctor's Experience with Lasers

Be sure to ask your doctor specific questions about his or her laser training. It's important to know the type of instrument he or she uses most frequently and how long he or she has been using it. Currently, all surgical residencies provide a good deal of practice with all forms of laser surgery, but older physicians trained thirty years ago may not be facile with them. They may not feel they need to learn a new technique at this point in their practice. Though some doctors state that laser laparoscopy is the only appropriate surgical treatment for endometriosis, it can present risks of perforation and bleeding, depending on the laser.

Be sure you're aware of your surgeon's skill and track record before you decide to go ahead with it. Many institutes offer physicians weekend courses in different types of laser surgery, but it takes years to master a specific technique with a specific instrument.

If you want laser surgery but your doctor doesn't do it, ask for a referral to someone who does.

OTHER PROCEDURES THAT MAY BE PERFORMED DURING A LAPAROSCOPY

Hysterosalpingogram

One of the most important tests to ascertain a woman's fertility is the hysterosalpingogram, which determines whether her fallopian tubes are open, or *patent.* In this procedure, a harmless dye, methylene blue, is injected up through the vagina into the uterus. If the fallopian tubes are open, the dye will continue up and pass through them; if they are blocked, no dye or only a small amount will pass through.

An added bonus to this procedure is it flushes out the cellular debris and menstrual reflux that collects in the tubes. This seems to help to relieve dysmenorrhea. It also seems to increase your chances of conceiving shortly after the laparoscopy (see Chapter 7).

Presacral and Uterosacral Neurectomy

The reproductive organs are held in place and secured to the spinal column in back by *presacral and uterosacral ligaments.* These ligaments are shot through with a branching system of nerves, which transmit sensations from throughout the pelvic cavity to the brain.

During a presacral neurectomy, the physician strips the nerves, which eliminates the transmission of pain messages. Some physicians routinely perform a presacral neurectomy during a laser laparoscopy if you suffer from chronic dysmenorrhea and haven't had any relief from previous medical treatment. The technique used to be performed only by surgeons exceptionally skilled with a scalpel; now it can be done more easily with a laser.

The presacral nerve filaments affect the contractile powers of the uterine muscle, so if your doctor removes them, you will no longer feel the cramping caused by the prostaglandin imbalance that is common in women with endometriosis.

Depending on where your endometrial implants are located, and depending on your surgeon's judgment, a similar procedure can be done on the uterosacral ligaments.

Some surgeons don't perform this procedure because they are concerned that it can lead to other problems later on. For example, in the first stage of labor you won't feel any contractions, and you may be unable to push after the transition.

Other doctors feel that it's important to give you as much pain relief as possible. But a woman who has had this neurectomy must be on a fetal monitor during her entire labor so that she and the medical staff can keep track of her contractions and stages of labor and know when to act.

Uterine Suspension

In this procedure, the uterosacral ligaments that hold the uterus and ovaries in place are tightened and shortened. The purpose of this is to keep them up and out of the way of the cul-de-sac, to make retrograde menstruation less likely. Some physicians do it routinely if you have moderate or severe disease involving the uterus and cul-de-sac. Others are more conservative in its use.

AFTER THE LAPAROSCOPY

Most physicians prescribe a six-to-nine-month course of hormonal suppression after a laparoscopy (see Chapter 6). Taking one of the various hormonal treatments is intended to "dry up" the microscopic areas the doctor may have missed during the laparoscopy. The various drug treatments also stop menses, which gives your body a rest from your periods. Without menstruation, new endometrial implants have much less opportunity to grow.

THE SECOND-LOOK LAPAROSCOPY

If you're still having symptoms after the course of medication is over, your physician will probably do a second-look laparoscopy to find out what the current state of your disease is. But if you have no symptoms after the course of medication, your physician will feel that the disease is under control, and you probably won't be scheduled for another appointment for about four to six months.

THE FUTURE OF
SURGICAL TREATMENT—
PELVISCOPIC SURGERY

Some physicians are now beginning to use a new technology known as *pelviscopic surgery*. The verdict is still out on its effectiveness, but it may hold promise for the treatment of endometriosis in the next decade.

The new instrument, the *pelviscope*, is a refinement of the laser laparoscope, and many physicians feel that it can do much more. Physicians well trained in this technology can remove anything from the pelvic cavity—even an endometrioma of nine to twelve millimeters—through a tiny laparoscopic incision. This is because the machine identifies and chops up the large cysts and sucks them out piecemeal.

Currently, this high-tech instrument is not widely available, and the surgeons familiar with its use are extremely few and far between. Some physicians do not favor the pelviscope because they feel that it is a harsher type of surgery than laparoscopy, requiring more punctures in the abdomen. It has been called "a laparotomy through the laparoscope." It is also more expensive because it is new.

As in any laser-laparoscopic surgery, the bleeding and adhesion-formation are minimal, hospital and operating-room time are short, and recovery is relatively easy.

But for now, most patients will continue to rely on their surgeon's ability to manage their disease with laparoscopy and laparotomy (see Chapter 8). As more doctors are better trained in the use of the various types of lasers, endometriosis surgery will become even more refined.

SIX

HORMONAL SUPPRESSION

One way to keep endometriosis under temporary control is to use drugs to alter your menstrual cycle. When your monthly cyclic pattern of bleeding and scarring is stopped, your implants are not hormonally stimulated. In fact, they may shrink, dry up, or disappear. This chapter discusses the various drug treatments used to manage the disease and explains their benefits and drawbacks.

Remember, no course of medication cures endometriosis—it only suppresses it. But hormonal therapy can help dramatically by limiting the progression of the disease and by reducing or eliminating its symptoms—at least for the period of time you're taking the medication.

The changeable nature of endometriosis depends on the monthly fluctuation of hormones in your body. The only times in a woman's life when the output of these hormones ceases naturally are during pregnancy and after menopause. But there are ways to create either a false pregnancy or a false menopause with drugs.

THE ENDOCRINE SYSTEM AND THE MENSTRUAL CYCLE

In order to understand how drug treatments work to control endometriosis, it's necessary to know a little about the body's endocrine system.

Hormones—from the Greek word meaning "to stimulate"—are chemical messengers that travel through the bloodstream and lymph system, relaying messages back and forth. Your hypothalamus, the "on switch" in the brain, produces a hormone called gonadotrophin-releasing hormone (GnRH), which triggers your pituitary gland to secrete follicle-stimulating hormone (FSH) and luteinizing hormone (LH).

In the first half of your monthly cycle, the *proliferative* or *follicular phase,* FSH stimulates the follicles, each of which contains an egg. The follicle puts out estrogen, which not only thickens the endometrium lining the uterus but encourages the growth of ectopic endometrial implants, adhesions, and endometriomas.

The second stage of your cycle is called the *luteal phase.* The variety of biochemical problems that can occur during this phase may be contributary factors to infertility—and many women who have endometriosis are often infertile (see Chapter 7). During this stage, a burst of LH from the pituitary stimulates ovulation and the production of the ovarian hormone *progesterone,* which builds up the endometrium into thicker and thicker layers as a possible home for an implanted egg. Estrogen is also secreted at this time and continues to "feed" the endometrial implants.

But if the egg doesn't get fertilized by a sperm, the estrogen and progesterone production dies off. Since the endometrium is no longer getting the hormonal support it needs to grow, within a matter of days, you shed it in the process called menstruation.

Unfortunately, the implants that were stimulated by the estrogen and progesterone have no outlet for shedding. They proliferate and swell with blood, then scar over. Each month, each cycle, gives them the hormonal opportunity to grow and allows new areas of involvement to develop.

Medical science can control the bleeding and scarring pattern of endometriosis by using artificial hormones to alter and stop your natural cycle. The current pharmacological treatments are as follows.

BIRTH CONTROL PILLS

If you have minimal to mild endometriosis, you can probably get complete relief by taking birth control pills *continuously.* You take a pill every day of the month—not for three weeks out of each month, as you would for contraceptive purposes. Birth control pills supply ovarian hormones to the body in a high progesterone-to-estrogen ratio, elevating the levels of these hormones in the blood and fooling the body into "believing" that a pregnancy has taken place.

When you take birth control pills continuously, you prevent the development of the egg. They also stop the endometrium from getting thicker, as well as the ectopic endometrial tissue. You have no menstrual debris to be shed, so you don't bleed.

Enovid is the drug most commonly used for this purpose in endometriosis, and it's taken at a low daily dose for six to nine months. Though it can't eradicate the endometrial implants you already have, it does prevent further growth. It is the most inexpensive treatment for endometriosis available, and it usually affords relief from pain and other symptoms of endometriosis. But it is not as effective as danazol in the treatment of infertility.

Side Effects

Not every woman has side effects from birth control pills, and most do not experience all of the following. But these are the side effects that it is possible to have:

- abdominal swelling
- breast tenderness
- nausea
- increased appetite
- edema
- breakthrough bleeding
- increased blood pressure
- blood clots

PROGESTOGENS

Progesterone, or the synthetic form (known as a *progestogen),* causes antimetabolic changes and stops ovulation from occurring. *Provera* (medroxyprogesterone acetate) is the drug most often prescribed, and it is given in either of two forms.

In the first form, as an intramuscular injection given every two weeks, the progestogen is known as *Depo-Provera.* An oral dose of estrogen is often taken with it for twenty-five days out of every month to control breakthrough bleeding. This regimen is usually maintained for four to five months. It can have long-lasting effects on your normal cycle, however, and it may take up to a year after your regimen is completed for ovulation to start up again. For this reason, Depo-Provera is not generally recommended if you want to attempt to get pregnant soon after the course of treatment.

But the second, oral form of the drug, Provera, seems to have a positive effect on your ability to conceive. It is taken daily for three to twelve months. Although it may take a few months for regular menstrual functioning to resume, at the end of this time fertility is very often enhanced. This progestogen regimen is currently very much in favor by the medical community in the treatment of minimal to mild endometriosis.

Side Effects

Although not every woman has side effects, it is possible to experience one or more of the following: edema, bloating, headaches, depression, and fatigue.

Oral contraceptives in any form are not recommended if you have large-cyst endometriomas. Both birth control pills and progestogens increase the growth of the cysts, which can then rupture, causing great pain and leakage of fluid. The scattering of all this endometrial debris can lead to more scar tissue and a worsening of your condition.

DANAZOL

Danazol (Danocrine) is the wonder drug of endometriosis treatment. It is probably the favorite of most physicians in the treatment of all but the most minimal forms of the disease. If you have mild to moderate endometriosis, it can be used alone or in conjunction with laparoscopic surgical treatment. If you suffer from severe endometriosis, it can be used pre- or postsurgically to treat your smaller lesions and implants. It will not, however, eradicate huge adhesions or large endometriomas.

Danazol is usually prescribed for six to nine months at a time, though some patients with greater tolerance to it report having been on it up to a year and a half. Unfortunately, its many unpleasant side effects prohibit continual use. Your regular menstrual cycle generally resumes about four to five weeks after the end of the treatment, but it may take longer.

Most doctors prescribe danazol at a dosage of 400 to 600 milligrams per day, divided into four doses. The dosage can be elevated to 800 milligrams daily if breakthrough bleeding occurs, and some patients may even need a slightly higher amount. Most physicians prefer to keep the dosage as low as possible while still maintaining the drug's effectiveness, because the greater the dosage, the more side effects you tend to have. Your doctor may experiment a bit with dosages to find the exact one that is right for you.

How Danazol Works

Danazol is a synthetic testosterone derivative. *Testosterone* is an androgen, or male hormone, that is produced naturally in very small amounts in the female body. It is responsible for the production of male secondary sex characteristics, such as a deepened voice, increased muscular development, and facial and pubic hair.

Danazol apparently disrupts the female hormonal cycle by suppressing the release of the pituitary hormones FSH and LH. In particular, it inhibits the surge of LH that triggers ovulation. It also suppresses the production of estrogen and progesterone.

While you are on danazol, your body is no longer subject to the hormonal fluctuations that perpetuate the growth of endometriosis. Without the monthly bleeding and scarring, your implants and lesions tend to "dry up." Some studies indicate that danazol lessens the production of the prostaglandins that contribute to dysmenorrhea. The drug may also have a beneficial effect on the immune system.

For those suffering from chronic pain, danazol is enormously effective. More than 90 percent of patients who have been on the medication report that their symptoms greatly lessened or vanished in the first month of treatment. And when used preoperatively on severe cases, physicians have reported that the lesions noticeably decreased in size since the initial laparoscopy. The drug does not seem to have a marked effect on endometriomas, however.

Unfortunately, after a course of danazol is over, there is no guarantee that your symptoms will not recur. Ten to 60 percent of all patients treated with danazol have to take another course of it a year to fifteen months after they stop. And other patients cannot complete even one course of danazol because they are so adversely affected by its side effects.

Contraindications

If your main purpose is to get pregnant, danazol is not a good course of treatment because time is lost during the months you're on the medication. You should not get pregnant while you are on danazol because the drug's high-potency hormones create a risk to the unborn fetus. To be certain that you don't conceive, your physician will prescribe a barrier form of contraception—a diaphragm or a condom, to be used with a spermicidal jelly or cream. You should use this contraceptive during your course of treatment and for a couple of months after it has ended, until the danazol is safely out of your system.

If you are not thinking of having a child for the next year or more, however, danazol may be a good choice for you. In one study pregnancy rates after a course of danazol increased from

30 to 53 percent—generally higher than the rates for women who have been on birth control pills. Most of the patients in the study were able to conceive within six months after the end of their treatment.

Some studies have found that danazol uses up the natural vitamin B_6 in your body. If you are on a course of treatment, you should ask your doctor whether he would advise you to take B_6 and/or additional B-complex vitamins. It is important that this vitamin be taken under medical supervision because an excess of it can produce nerve damage.

Side Effects

As a masculinizing hormone, danazol produces physical characteristics that may be intolerable to you. About 85 percent of all patients experience *some* of the following side effects:

- weight gain (muscle bulk, as opposed to fat, which is difficult to lose)

- decreased breast size

- muscle cramps

- hot flashes

- oily skin and hair

- acne

- coarse hair growth

- deepened or hoarse voice

- enlarged clitoris

- decreased or increased libido (highly variable)

- nausea

- headache

- fatigue

- insomnia

- carpal tunnel syndrome (pain, tingling, or numbness in fingers or arm)

- lowered HDLs (the "good" cholesterol)

- liver dysfunction

It may be several months after the end of your treatment before the masculinizing effects of danazol lessen, and some of the changes that have occurred in your body may never reverse. Some women report that their voices remain deep and hoarse and that the coarse hair that grew on their stomach, upper thighs, or face could only be removed by electrolysis. Most patients, though anxious about these side effects, are willing to tolerate them because of the effectiveness of the drug on their pain and other symptoms.

If you've been losing up to four days a month from work, if you cannot enjoy sexual intercourse, or if you're exhausted from coping with depression and hopelessness about your chronic condition, you will probably find this hormonal treatment is life-enhancing and generally beneficial.

Costs

Danazol, which is sold under the brand name Danocrine, costs about $150 to $200 per month. But if you call the various pharmacies in your area, you may find one or two that carry generic brands, which cost as little as $122 per month. Check with your insurance company to find out whether you're covered, and to what extent.

GNRH ANALOGS

GnRH is the trigger of the whole menstrual cycle. Medical science has developed an analog or man-made version of this hormone to treat certain cancers, and it also works effectively on endometriosis.

How GnRH Works

GnRH, as we have seen, is released in a pulsing fashion from the hypothalamus, causing the pituitary to put out FSH and LH. These, in turn, act on the ovaries to put out estrogen, which influences the proliferation of endometrial tissue. If you have endometriosis, of course, it is not only the lining of your uterus that grows under the influence of estrogen but the endometriosis implants and lesions elsewhere in your body as well.

Natural GnRH stimulates the pituitary, and its pulsing action encourages FSH and LH production. But when the man-made analog is given *continuously,* its effect is just the opposite. It desensitizes the pituitary, suppressing its hormones, which means that the menstrual cycle never gets started.

Without FSH and LH, no estrogen or progesterone is produced, and there is no ovulation or growth of endometrial tissue. It is as if the ovaries are not there at all. For this reason the treatment is often referred to as "medical oophorectomy." (An oophorectomy is the surgical removal of the ovaries.)

These analogs are manufactured under several brand names such as Synarel and Lupron. Although Lupron was originally developed as a treatment for men with prostate cancer, the drug has recently gained FDA approval in its repackaged form, in dosages appropriate for women with endo.

The Synarel nasal spray form is to be used twice daily in each nostril. It is easy to use and has been shown to be only slightly less effective than the depo form of Lupron, which is injected subcutaneously once a month.

GnRH-analog therapy is enormously effective in mild to moderate cases of endometriosis. GnRH analogs also shrink large endometriomas in severe cases, which make them more operable. Like danazol, GnRH analogs have no effect on adhesions and scar tissue.

The treatment is generally administered for six months or so and offers great relief of symptoms with substantially fewer side effects than danazol.

Contraindications

Estrogen helps the body absorb calcium and therefore allows bone tissue to be remodeled continually throughout life up to menopause. At menopause, demineralization begins to occur, which can lead to osteoporosis. Estrogen also tends to increase the HDL levels in blood (the "good" cholesterol) and to decrease the LDL ("bad" cholesterol) levels.

The biggest drawback of GnRH analogs is that they deprive the body of estrogen, creating a state similar to menopause. GnRH-analog therapy, over time, may prove damaging to the bones and heart in ways that remain unclear.

There are no statistics yet on how fertility is affected after the cessation of the drug. But the menstrual cycle usually starts right up again, and there is usually no significant waiting time before conception is possible. As with danazol, once you're off the medication, you do risk a recurrence of the disease.

Side Effects

The side effects from GnRH analogs that some patients have are identical to those experienced by women going through menopause. They include:

- hot flashes
- vaginal atrophy and itching
- demineralization
- increased LDLs; lowered HDLs
- breakthrough bleeding
- mild joint stiffness or soreness
- insomnia
- fatigue
  The Synarel nasal spray occasionally causes nasal congestion in some women.

Costs of GnRH

The cost of either the Synarel spray or the depo Lupron is about $300 a month.

A second type of dosage comes as a daily twenty-eight-day kit, which costs about $300 to $350. You must learn to use a syringe and inject yourself, as a diabetic learns to inject insulin.

PAIN MEDICATION

If you have finished a course of danazol or GnRH analog and are starting to have a recurrence of symptoms but it's too soon to start another course of hormonal therapy, most physicians will try to maintain you on *nonsteroidal anti-inflammatory drugs (NSAIDs)*.

Remember that any pain-killer can be habit-forming and should be used only under a doctor's supervision—even if it's available over the counter.

NSAIDs can be effective in the control of endometriosis pain. Ibuprofin, which comes in over-the-counter versions (such as Motrin, Advil, or Nuprin) and by prescription (Anaprox, Meclomen, or Ansaid), is a NSAID that is a prostaglandin inhibitor. It stops the contraction of smooth muscle tissue that is partly responsible for the agonizing pain of dysmenorrhea. NSAIDs also provide protection against inflammation. This means that they are very good for lower back pain and cramping in your joints.

You can take *aspirin* and its derivatives instead, but aspirin is not as effective against pain and has a variety of unpleasant gastrointestinal side effects. Aspirin also interferes with blood clotting, causing you to bleed and bruise more easily. *Acetaminophen* interferes with prostaglandin production, which is good, since it controls cramping. But it has no anti-inflammatory effects. Combination products that contain both aspirin and acetaminophen include Midol, Pamprin, and Cope.

For relief of crippling pain, some doctors will give you a prescription for a *narcotic,* such as codeine, Darvocet, or Percodan. Narcotics may be effective on a short-term basis, but the body soon becomes tolerant of a particular dosage. This means that you need to take them in increasingly greater amounts to receive pain relief. Narcotics create psychological dependence, too, as well as a variety of side effects such as dizziness, shortness of breath, increased heart rate, hives, itching, and insomnia.

If you are currently on danazol or GnRH analogs but are still having so much pain that you need to take a pain medication, check with your doctor. Something may be wrong with the dosage of your hormonal treatment. The particular course of treatment you're on may not be right for the severity of your disease. If your doctor tells you that the birth control pills he's prescribed will work "eventually" and that you should just be patient, see another physician.

In some instances, however, you may experience pain even though you are under adequate medical supervision. If you are between surgical or medical treatments and begin to have some symptoms again, you may fear that they will get worse. That fear itself may create enough stress to exacerbate your pain. Here are some steps you can take to avoid or lessen pain before it becomes crippling:

1. Keep your endometriosis diary up-to-date. Be aware of your body. Note in the diary whether the pain remains the same, diminishes, or increases while you're in the midst of your period, and whether it's in the same location as it was the month before or a different one. Write down all other symptoms and whether they get better or worse from month to month.

2. If you are on a regimen of birth control pills, progestogens, danazol, or GnRH analogs, mark down in your diary when you started and at what dosage, and when and if your dosage was changed. Indicate any and all changes in symptoms chronologically. Note whether they coincide with changes in your medications.

3. Make a check mark in the diary whenever your premenstrual dysmenorrhea begins. If you experience pain only during your period, make the check mark a day before it's likely to start. If you typically begin having pain at another point in your cycle, begin taking a NSAID *before* that point. NSAIDs should be taken according to the package instructions, or as your doctor recommends.

4. If you are at all confused about what's happening in your body, check in with your doctor by phone between appointments. Sometimes a change in your dosage is all that's necessary to keep your endometriosis under control.

5. There are a variety of professional organizations around the country that can assist you in pain management. See Chapter 11 for a full discussion of these groups, and Chapter 10 for other ways to manage pain and related symptoms.

SEVEN

INFERTILITY

Infertility, which is the inability to conceive a child after a year of unprotected sexual relations, is one of the major symptoms of endometriosis. In this chapter we explore how the disease affects fertility and the options available to you for trying to become pregnant.

Infertile women are seven to ten times more likely to have endometriosis than fertile women, but this doesn't necessarily mean that endometriosis *causes* infertility. Nor does the currently popular choice to delay childbearing cause endometriosis. Delay simply gives your body years of uninterrupted cycling, which can create a hormonal environment where endometrial implants can grow and proliferate.

Some physicians believe that women who have Stage I or Stage II endo may in fact have a combination of several physical and biochemical problems that contribute to their difficulties in becoming and staying pregnant. In one study women who had minimal endometriosis had no greater success at conceiving twelve months after being treated with danazol than those who had had no treatment at all. This indicates that alleviating their endometriosis had no effect on their fertility.

Your entire medical history plays a part in your fertility picture. If you used birth control pills for contraception during the years when you were single or establishing your career, they may well have masked your endometriosis. The effect of the Pill is to thin out the endometrium, causing less menstrual debris to be shed—a lighter menstrual flow—and therefore less chance of retrograde menstruation. If this is the case, only when you decided to conceive and went off the Pill did your endometriosis become apparent.

IS IT HARDER TO GET PREGNANT NOW THAN IT USED TO BE?

One of the great ironies of endo is that by the time you decide to have a child, you may not be able to. There are so many possible reasons for infertility that no one is exactly sure what mechanism prevents conception and successful pregnancy. But it is a fact that endometriosis is responsible for part of the high infertility statistics in the United States today. Fifteen percent of couples in the United States are currently considered infertile; of these, about 10 percent have endo as the *only* demonstrable cause. And 30 percent of all women diagnosed with endometriosis are infertile.

The statistics on infertility have become widely publicized in the last ten years, and people talk about the problem much more freely. It is actually not true that more couples are infertile, but the demographics of infertility have changed. More older couples today are having difficulty having babies.

Why is this so? The first reason is that as you age, the number of viable eggs in your ovaries decreases. If you wait until your late thirties or early forties to try to conceive, you have that many fewer chances.

Some couples today may be paying dearly for the sexual experimentation of the 1960s, when "free love" was the norm. The more sexual partners a person has had, the greater his or her chances of contracting a sexually transmitted disease. The longer such diseases go untreated, the more devastating the consequences may be. Even wearing an IUD can set up an infection that may permanently damage tubes and ovaries, making it impossible for you to conceive.

WHY ENDOMETRIOSIS MAY CONTRIBUTE TO INFERTILITY

In order to conceive a child, a couple must engage in sexual relations around the time of ovulation, when the fertilized egg is on its way to the uterus. But if you have endometriosis, many factors may contribute to your difficulty in conceiving. These factors include the following:

Pain

- If intercourse is terribly painful, you may avoid having sexual relations.

Mechanical Problems

- Adhesions may block the egg from passing from ovary to tube to uterus. The tube may adhere to the abdomen and may not be able to move and grasp the egg as it is released from the ovary. If you have adhesions inside the tubes, they can prevent the egg from traveling from the ovary to the tube to the uterus. Even if conception does take place, it may happen inside the tube, resulting in an ectopic pregnancy, which is extremely dangerous and must be terminated.

- Anatomical distortion, which is relatively common in women with endometriosis, may prevent normal passage of the egg. If the uterus is tipped backward and fixed in place by adhesions or if the cervix is displaced, it will be more difficult for the sperm to make a direct journey upward.

Problems with Ovulation

- You may have irregular menses, which makes it difficult for you to know when you are ovulating.

- You may not be ovulating at all.

- You may be having problems with the second half of your cycle. If you have a "luteal phase defect," the supply of progesterone produced after ovulation is inadequate. (Progesterone is the hormone that helps to provide the rich, dense endometrium in which the fertilized egg can grow.)

- You may have "unruptured follicle syndrome," in which the egg is never expelled from the ovary although all the hormones are being produced.

Prostaglandins

- Prostaglandins are fatty-acid derivatives created in the endometrium and also in ectopic endometriosis implants. These hormonelike substances help cause the smooth muscles of the uterus to contract. This contraction is felt as a menstrual cramp. Women with endometriosis tend to produce more prostaglandins in their peritoneal fluid, which can make their tubes contract, bringing the egg down to the uterus too quickly. Bad timing might prevent the meeting of ovum and sperm. Also, if the egg is rushed along its journey, it may be too immature to implant when it arrives at the uterine wall.

- In some studies, the prostaglandins in women with endo have been suspected of interfering with the ability of the ovaries to release an egg.

Autoimmune Response

- An immune-system deficiency may be at least partially responsible for endometriosis (see Chapter 2).

- Women with endometriosis, it has been found, have an abundance of peritoneal fluid, and theirs contains a higher percentage of *macrophages* (white blood cells known as "clean-up cells") than the peritoneal fluid of women without endo. One of the functions of macrophages is to destroy invaders. That means they kill sperm cells.

- The peritoneal fluid in women with endometriosis may also prevent egg capture by the oviductal fimbria—the fingerlike protrusions at the ends of the fallopian tubes. This may have implications for problems with fertilization and embryo growth.

- Macrophages secrete a hormone, called interleukin-1, that increases the body's production of collagen, a kind of protein that is present in connective tissue. Collagen keeps your skin firm and young looking, but it is also responsible for the proliferation of scar tissue in the abdomen.

Spontaneous Abortion

- Spontaneous abortions, due to a short luteal phase, occur in more than half the women with endo who do manage to conceive. Women with endometriosis have a three times greater risk of miscarrying early in their pregnancy than women who don't have the disease.

THE INFERTILITY WORKUP

The purpose of the infertility workup is to isolate the specific cause or causes of your difficulty conceiving. Your physician will begin by asking you how long you and your partner have been having unprotected sex, how regular your attempts at intercourse are, and whether you've had relations at various times of the month. If it has been at least a year since you started trying to conceive, you are considered to have fertility problems.

The doctor will then order a *semen analysis,* a sperm count and viability test for your partner, to determine whether he has any physical complications that are interfering with conception.

Your physician will ask you to keep a *basal body temperature chart.* You are to take your temperature before getting out of bed each morning and record it on the chart. A surge in progesterone level raises your basal body temperature, so your temperature will rise a few points after ovulation and stay this high until just before menstruation. A chart kept over several months will tell the doctor whether you're ovulating, when your ovulation occurs, and how long the second half (luteal phase) of your cycle lasts.

If your basal body temperature is erratic, your doctor may ask you to use an *ovulation predictor test.* This home test turns color approximately twenty-four hours before you ovulate, about twelve or thirteen days before you start to menstruate. It's important for your doctor to know when your period begins so that he or she can check the progesterone level during your luteal phase.

The doctor will do a *blood test* to check your thyroid level, as well as your levels of FSH, LH, prolactin, and testosterone. He or she will check your progesterone level after you've ovulated.

Two to three days before your predicted period, the doctor

will take an *endometrial biopsy,* a small segment of tissue that is removed vaginally from the endometrium. He or she will examine it under a microscope to see whether the amount of endometrial growth present is in sync with your menstrual cycle.

You and your partner will also be asked to take a *postcoital test* a few hours after sexual relations. This will tell the doctor how thick your cervical mucus is and whether your partner's sperm can pass through it.

Your doctor may recommend that you have a *hysterosalpingo-gram.* In this test, dye is injected into the uterus and traced up through the tubes (see Chapter 5). An X ray is then taken to see whether the tubes are open (or "patent"). If you have no blockage from adhesions or twisted organs, the dye will flow through freely, then disperse through the pelvic cavity.

Some women with a history of fertility problems get pregnant after having this test, although scientists are unsure why it would help conception. It may have something to do with clearing out menstrual debris that might be clinging to the cilia lining your tubes.

All these tests are performed in a fertility workup on any woman who is unable to become pregnant, regardless of whether her physician suspects endometriosis. Many women who come in for a fertility workup have never experienced pain with menses or intercourse. They are therefore unprepared when their doctor tells them that he can feel rosary bead nodules or a pelvic mass and would like to order a laparoscopy to check for endometriosis. The *laparoscopy* (see Chapter 5), may include an option to laser, excise, or cauterize any implants or lesions and to attempt to free up blockages around your tubes and ovaries.

Fortunately, endometriosis usually affects only the outside of the fallopian tubes and other organs. Except in very rare cases, the adhesions and implants grow around organs, leaving the inside healthy. Therefore, women with endo stand a greater chance of conceiving than do women with PID, or damage from an infection set up by an IUD, which tends to affect the insides of the tubes.

TREATMENTS FOR INFERTILITY

If your goal is to conceive as soon as possible, your physician will first attempt to correct any mechanical problems surgically, usually by lasering or cutting away adhesions and implants during a laparoscopy.

If your endometriosis is severe, and adhesions or a large endometrioma has obstructed your ovaries or tubes, you may need more extensive surgery to reconstruct your pelvic anatomy. A course of progestogens, danazol, or GnRH analogs is sometimes used before a laparotomy (see Chapter 8) to try to reduce as much of the endometriosis as possible before surgery. Another course of medication may be ordered after surgery, depending on how quickly you want to become pregnant. You and your doctor will make this decision based on your age and how many reproductive years remain to you.

If you have minimal to mild endometriosis and you wish to have a baby as soon as possible, your doctor will probably recommend no pre- or postoperative hormonal treatment.

If, after another six or eight months, you still have not conceived, your doctor may wish to put you on a medication that will induce ovulation, first clomiphene citrate (Clomid), and if that fails, human menopausal gonadotrophin (Pergonal). These drugs regulate your cycle and stimulate the production and fertilization of eggs. (It should be noted that Pergonal treatment does have mood-altering side effects and has been known to produce multiple births.)

HAVING ENDOMETRIOSIS DOESN'T MEAN YOU CAN'T HAVE A BABY

Many women with Stage I or Stage II endometriosis will be able to have a child after receiving proper hormonal and/or surgical treatment. For those with more serious forms of the disease, the outlook is less optimistic.

Still, as long as you have one viable piece of ovary from which a physician can extract an egg, you need not give up all hope of becoming pregnant. Thanks to techniques that medical science has developed, improved, and expanded to enhance or artificially engineer fertility, endometriosis need no longer doom you to being childless.

If you have not conceived after eighteen months to two years of other treatments for infertility, your physician may suggest that you and your husband or partner consider in vitro fertilization—embryo transfer (IVF/ET) or gamete intrafallopian transfer (GIFT).

In Vitro Fertilization—Embryo Transfer (IVF/ET)

This procedure is used if you have damaged fallopian tubes but at least a piece of one healthy ovary. If you are selected for IVF, you are given GnRH analogs as well as fertility drugs to mature several ova at once. These are removed from your ovary during a laparoscopy or retrieved through the vagina by using ultrasound. The ova are placed in a glass dish, where they are fertilized by your spouse's or a donor's semen. If fertilization occurs, after about a three-day wait to ensure development, the ova are put back into your uterus with a catheter, and you are given progesterone to support the pregnancy.

Gamete Intrafallopian Transfer (GIFT)

This procedure is used if you have at least one tube and ovary intact. The ova are matured and removed, as in IVF, then are mixed with sperm obtained earlier. They are immediately replaced to the opening of the fallopian tube using the laparoscope. Fertilization can then occur in the body, as it might have naturally.

This is a rather new procedure, and although it is neither as difficult nor as expensive as IVF, it is not widely available.

Costs and Risks

To become a candidate for IVF or GIFT, you have to be accepted by a university hospital whose staff is experienced in these techniques. You must be prepared to handle large expenses that are generally not covered by insurance and to spend a great deal of time; most important, you must be prepared for possible disappointment.

Each cycle of IVF costs $5,000 to $6,000, and it usually takes four to six attempts to achieve conception. Couples whose infertility is caused only by mild to moderate endometriosis tend to have higher success rates than those with other or unknown reasons for their infertility. Still, only 20 percent of couples who use IVF are actually able to carry a baby to term. The statistics on GIFT are as yet too small to give us a realistic assessment of its success.

If you enter one of these programs, it is very important that you do so with a realistic awareness of your chances. If all attempts at biological reproduction fail, you still have the option of adopting a child. And you can obviously keep trying to conceive even after adoption.

THE BENEFITS OF PREGNANCY,
IF YOU ACHIEVE IT

Doctors used to suggest pregnancy as a cure for endometriosis because it temporarily suspends the menstrual cycle. But since we now know that endometriosis is caused by many factors—only one of which is hormonal fluctuation—pregnancy is no longer regarded as a panacea. Women with endo tend to experience harder pregnancies, more miscarriages, harder labors, and more severe postpartum depression than women who don't have the disease. And in rare cases endometriosis worsens during pregnancy.

In most situations, however, if you're able to become pregnant, you may get some relief from your symptoms. Because your cycling has stopped and you do not bleed and scar on a monthly basis, there is less opportunity for ectopic endometrial tissue to proliferate. If you are one of the fortunate ones for whom pregnancy does offer temporary remission, you can give your body a well-needed rest as you happily prepare to welcome your child to the world.

If your endometriosis symptoms return shortly after your menses resume (as is very often the case), you should seek medical help at once. Some studies have shown that it may be easier for you to conceive a second or third time if you have good endometriosis management after your first child is weaned. Other studies, however, show that some women have difficulty attempting subsequent pregnancies, possibly because they weren't treated after the birth of their first child. If you don't seek medical attention in between pregnancies, you have no way of knowing whether your cycling is encouraging the growth of new endometrial tissue.

Some cases of complete remission from the disease after pregnancy have been reported. Although medical science cannot yet explain why a pregnancy could alter a woman's whole hormonal picture, it is nonetheless possible for a fortunate few to break the pattern of this chronic illness.

EIGHT

SURGICAL TREATMENTS

Open surgery is a major but common step in the treatment of endometriosis. If your previous laparoscopies and medical treatments have failed to improve your symptoms, your doctor will probably recommend a laparotomy. If not even a laparotomy gives you relief of unbearable symptoms and if your childbearing years are over, you may ultimately decide on radical surgery (hysterectomy) or definitive surgery (oophorectomy). This chapter explains what these operations entail and details their risks and benefits.

LAPAROTOMY

In a laparotomy the abdominal cavity is opened with a half-moon-shaped incision, about four or five inches in length, made through the abdominal muscle. The doctor makes this incision above the pubic hairline, or "bikini line." The intestines and bladder, previously drained with a catheter, are clamped aside so that the surgeon can fully explore your reproductive organs for implants, lesions, and growths.

When Is a Laparotomy Recommended?

A laparotomy may be suggested if your symptoms have persistently recurred after several laser laparoscopies and after various hormonal regimens have been tried.

You might also be a candidate for a laparotomy if:

- you have a very large endometrioma that must be removed

- you have a lot of involvement in delicate or difficult-to-reach areas such as the cul-de-sac or the urinary and gastrointestinal tracts

- your adhesions are freezing all your pelvic organs in place

- your doctor must reconstruct your pelvic anatomy and restore your organs to their normal place and function

- your doctor must repair damage done to your tubes and ovaries in order to enhance your fertility

- distorted organs are pressing on your bladder or bowel. In time this can become a life-threatening condition.

"Conservative" Surgery

Laparotomy is called conservative surgery because it conserves your ability to bear children. Some doctors call it conservative even if they must remove damaged pelvic structures. As long as the uterus and one ovary and fallopian tube can be retained, thus preserving the possibility of natural conception and childbirth, it is considered conservative. And as long as one healthy piece of an ovary is retained, it is still possible for you to have a child through in vitro fertilization or gamete intrafallopian transfer (see Chapter 7).

Laparotomy and Infertility

Some cases of endometriosis are so severe that the doctor can tell during the initial laparoscopy that open surgery is required. In other cases several laser laparoscopies and several courses of hormonal suppression are attempted first. A lot also depends on your biological clock and your timetable for conceiving. If you are anxious about losing precious childbearing years and you have Stage III or Stage IV endometriosis, you might be counseled to have it surgically treated as soon as possible.

Statistics show that fertility rates in women with *severe* endometriosis improve more dramatically after open surgery (or open surgery preceded by a course of danazol or GnRH analogs) than after hormonal treatment without surgery.

Some doctors prefer to do a laparotomy only after you undergo a six-to-nine-month course of hormonal suppression to shrink or dry up some of the implants. Others feel that danazol or GnRH analogs may soften the cysts and increase the likelihood that they will rupture. You should discuss your own situation at length with your physician.

Before You Go to the Hospital

The medical testing and presurgery preparation for your laparotomy will be the same as for a therapeutic laparoscopy (see Chapter 5), but since this is abdominal surgery, the recovery time will be longer and more difficult.

It's always helpful to inform yourself about your surgery and hospital procedures as much as possible *before* you're admitted. Ask your doctor for any brochures or fact sheets he may have on laparotomies, and call the hospital to see if they have a patient information tour or class. It's good to know beforehand whether your pubic area will have to be shaved prior to surgery, or if you will need an additional ultrasound or intestinal examination, or how long you'll be fed and medicated intravenously after your operation. Some hospitals allow you to visit the operating room and see the equipment and instruments that will be used.

At least a week before your surgery, you should start getting more rest and building up your strength. This may mean going to bed an hour earlier, stopping smoking, and eating a healthful diet. Some bowel preparation will be ordered beginning several days before your surgery if you have extensive disease in the bowel or sigmoid colon. This requires a liquid diet, ingestion of citrate of magnesia, and enemas (see Chapter 5).

You'll be asked to sign a consent form before surgery, indicating that you agree to allow your doctor to perform whatever procedures you've previously discussed. Be sure to read this form carefully, because you'll undoubtedly be nervous and preoccupied before you go to the operating room. Sign the form *only* if it follows your personal choices.

You'll be sedated in your room and brought to the operating room, where general anesthesia will be administered.

The Operation

Some surgeons begin by dilating the cervix to allow as much passage as possible for the endometrial debris that will accumulate postsurgically and to cut down on the maximum amount of retrograde flow.

After making his incision, your physician will remove any superficial implants and lesions on the peritoneum that may be hiding underlying disease. If your endometriosis has glued organs together or twisted them out of shape, the surgeon's first job will be to separate them and put them back in place. He will do this with scalpel, cautery, or laser—whatever technique he considers most useful in a particular site.

Next, your doctor will explore the entire pelvic area for implants and lesions, sometimes using an optical loupe for microsurgical magnification.

The surgeon will inject dye through the fallopian tubes to see how much blockage there is. If *tuboplasty,* or reconstruction of a tube, is necessary, this will be done with microsurgical techniques. If the tube is severely damaged, it may be removed.

An *ovarian wedge resection* may be done if you have extensive disease on one or both ovaries. In this procedure the diseased part of the ovary is cut away and sutured or stapled closed after all visible signs of endometriosis have been removed. If the surgeon decides that your endometriomas are too large or extensive to be removed or if they're obstructing blood supply to an ovary, he may have to remove the ovary itself. It's possible that one ovary and tube will have severe disease, yet the other may be completely untouched by endometriosis. If this is your situation, your chances of conceiving may still be quite good.

A *bowel resection* may be done if you have extensive disease in the bowel or sigmoid colon.

A *uterine suspension* may be performed to tighten and lift the ligaments attaching the uterus to the pelvic cavity. It is also helpful in cases where the uterus has been frozen into place by extensive endometriosis in the cul-de-sac. It's also useful if adhesions have glued the ovaries to other pelvic organs.

A *presacral or uterosacral neurectomy* may be performed with a scalpel or laser to sever the nerves that transmit pain messages to the brain (see Chapter 5).

What Happens after Conservative Surgery?

There is no guarantee that your symptoms will not recur after surgery. Endometriosis is a disease that is always in flux, and implants that were microscopic at the time of your surgery may grow within six months, or a new area may appear to be affected. The reason for this is that as long as you have your ovaries, you are still producing estrogen and progesterone—and therefore you are still stimulating the growth of endometriosis tissue.

Most physicians feel it wisest to follow up conservative surgery with a six-to-nine-month course of danazol or GnRH analogs (see Chapter 6). This will ensure that smaller implants will dry up and that new ones will not be allowed to proliferate. Great improvement and occasional remissions have been reported from a combination of surgical and medical management, even in moderate to severe cases of endometriosis.

You may be scheduled for a second-look laparoscopy about four months after your laparotomy. Many physicians, concerned that scar tissue may result after open surgery has healed, want to take another look inside after the course of medication has had a chance to do its work. During this laparoscopy the surgeon will be able to see how effective the combined surgical and hormonal treatments have been and whether there are any new areas of involvement. Any adhesions that were formed from cutting and suturing can now be vaporized by laser.

Fertility after Laparotomy

Fertility immediately after conservative surgery is often enhanced. For this reason, if you wish to become pregnant, your doctor may advise you to try to do so as soon as you have recuperated. Fertility rates tend to decline the longer you wait to conceive after a laparotomy.

RADICAL SURGERY
AND DEFINITIVE SURGERY

Removing the uterus, ovaries, and fallopian tubes to "cure" endometriosis is recommended only for women who have no further interest in childbearing and whose symptoms persist despite all other types of treatment.

Many endometriosis patients with severe, chronic disease feel enormous relief once they have had this surgery. Unfortunately, others have persistent pain even after the operation.

Having your reproductive organs removed is an extremely serious step to take, and you should discuss the ramifications carefully with your physician and your family. You should get a second opinion if definitive surgery is advised—most insurance companies insist on it.

Radical surgery or *total hysterectomy* would occur only if initial surgery and drug treatments still leave you incapacitated by pain and, possibly, by life-threatening organ obstruction. In radical surgery your uterus and cervix are removed, as well as adhesions, implants, and cysts on other areas in the pelvic cavity.

Many physicians report high recurrence rates for the disease if the ovaries are not removed. For this reason fewer hysterectomies are being done now because they are not radical enough to treat severe forms of endometriosis.

Definitive surgery, or *total abdominal hysterectomy and bilateral salpingo-oophorectomy (TAHBSO),* involves the removal of *all* reproductive organs—uterus, cervix, and both ovaries and fallopian tubes, as well as lesions, implants, and cysts on other areas such as the bowel, bladder, or cul-de-sac. If you have a "clean-out," as it's commonly known, you will immediately go through premature menopause.

The feeling most prevalent in the medical community right now is that only by castration—taking out the uterus, tubes, and ovaries—do you have the best chance of a complete remission. With the source of estrogen and progesterone gone from the body, there's no further opportunity for hormonal stimulation of your implants. There is still no guarantee that an oophorectomy will effect a "cure" in every case, however, because there are many other factors involved in endometriosis.

Disadvantages of Oophorectomy

Although an oophorectomy may have an extremely beneficial effect on your life, it does have certain risks and drawbacks.

Without your ovaries you will be in a state of estrogen deficiency. Estrogen has a protective effect on your bones because it ensures the absorption of calcium in your body. You will be at greater risk for developing osteoporosis because you will experience a slow but steady decrease in bone tissue mass after an oophorectomy.

You will also be at higher risk for heart disease because you've lost the protective effects of estrogen on your lipoproteins, lowering your HDLs (the "good" cholesterol) and raising your LDLs (the "bad" cholesterol).

You will experience a variety of menopausal symptoms, such as hot flashes and vaginal dryness and itching, and perhaps also a temporary lessening of your sex drive.

If you are a young woman in your thirties or forties when you have this surgery, you have that many more years of estrogen deficiency ahead of you and that much greater opportu-

nity to suffer menopausal symptoms or develop heart disease
or osteoporosis.

Estrogen Replacement Therapy (ERT)
after Surgical Menopause

Should you take artificial estrogen to relieve the menopausal
symptoms that will occur when your ovaries are removed?
Doctors are of two opinions. Since estrogen is one of the major
factors responsible for the development of endometriosis,
many physicians feel that it's unwise to put you on estrogen
replacement therapy (ERT).

If your physician is opposed to giving you estrogen after a
oophorectomy, there are other ways of dealing with your
menopausal symptoms. The drug Depo-Provera, a progestogen, successfully suppresses hot flashes and also allows any
residual endometriosis to regress.

Other physicians feel that ERT is appropriate for oophorec-
tomized patients if some time has passed after surgery and all
hormonal cycling has stopped. They feel that the artificial hormones will not restimulate your endometriosis if they are given
continuously rather than cyclically. A conservative length of
time to wait postsurgically is six to nine months. (You can be
maintained on Depo-Provera up to this point.) After half a year
or a little more, you can be reasonably certain that all traces of
endo are gone.

If you begin to have any recurrence of symptoms, your physician may stop the ERT. If he or she suspects any growth of
ectopic endometrial tissue, Lupron or danazol may be prescribed for three or four months. Or he or she may decide to
take you off all medication, carefully monitoring your condition
during this time.

Recuperating after Surgery

Both radical and definitive surgery require considerable recovery time, both physically and psychologically. You will be in the hospital for about a week, and you will need some help with personal maintenance and with household chores after you are discharged from the hospital. Once you are home, you should call your doctor if:

- your incision becomes red and inflamed or is oozing mucus

- you have chills or fever

- you have severe abdominal pain

- you have side effects from any medication prescribed post-surgically.

A laparotomy requires about a four-to-six-week recuperation period. Depending on the type of work you do, you may be advised to take a month's leave after surgery. Sexual intercourse and rigorous exercise are prohibited for six weeks after surgery.

A hysterectomy or oophorectomy may require longer recuperation, but it also may not. Some women report feeling back to normal after a month, but for others, it may take almost a year to recover both physically and emotionally. Regardless of how you feel, however, you will be counseled to take it easy for at least six weeks. You should not do any lifting over five pounds, and avoid making beds and climbing stairs. You will find that you are much more tired than usual during the day.

After any major surgery, the key is to get your strength back slowly. You should eat a nutritious diet of small meals and do only the exercises your doctor prescribes. Remember that you may feel wonderful and tend to overdo one day, then feel completely exhausted the next.

If you've had a hysterectomy or oophorectomy, you will also

have psychological problems to deal with. Many women report terrible depression, a feeling that they've lost their femininity, and a lack of sexual interest even after physical recuperation. All these emotions are understandable and completely normal.

If your physician does not feel capable of counseling you about the emotional aspects of recovery, you may wish to consult a psychologist or social worker. Often, just a few visits can make a big difference in your perspective. It can also be enormously helpful to join an endometriosis or hysterectomy support group in your area (see Chapter 11).

NINE

EARLY AND LATE ENDOMETRIOSIS:
Teenagers and Older Women

Although most endometriosis patients are women in their late twenties and early thirties, more and more teenagers and older —even postmenopausal—women are being diagnosed with the disease. The fact that so many women of different backgrounds suffer from endometriosis seems to indicate that there are many contributory factors to the condition. In fact, what we call endometriosis may be many diseases.

TEENAGERS

The most common theory explaining why endometriosis occurs is retrograde menstruation. But it has been shown that it takes about five years of bleeding and scarring before implants and endometriomas cause serious pain and internal dysfunctioning. It doesn't seem to make good scientific sense that a thirteen- or fourteen-year-old with only a couple of years of cycling behind her should have the crippling symptoms of the disease.

We must therefore consider other possible contributory factors.

- Heredity. Endometriosis is more likely to appear in members of the same family on the maternal side. If a girl's mother, aunt, or cousin has the disease, there is a good chance that she may get it. The onset of menses may stimulate dormant ectopic endometrial cells that have existed since birth.

- Transmigration from the blood or lymph system. Endo may not need a fully developed hormonal system to proliferate. Cases of endo have been diagnosed in the lungs and armpits, where there is no hormonal activity.

- Autoimmune imbalance. A young girl may have a deficiency in her autoimmune system that allows foreign tissue to be accepted as host tissue.

Most older women, when asked when their symptoms first began, report that they experienced pain for years before ever seeking help. They just assumed the problem would go away in time or that they would get used to it. Instead, what happened was that their endometriosis grew and worsened, year after year. For this reason, it is doubly important to inform teenagers and their parents of the benefits of early detection.

The Benefits of Early Detection

If you are a teenager and you have unusually bad periods that make it difficult or impossible for you to concentrate at school or to participate in extracurricular activities, *you should see a gynecologist.* The earlier endometriosis is detected and the sooner you get treatment, the better are your chances of having a pain-free existence and little difficulty conceiving a child later in your life.

If you are in pain and discomfort every month, you should discuss the situation with your mother or another woman you trust, even if you find it embarrassing to do so. You may be surprised to learn that your mother, sister, or aunt has some of the same symptoms—even if they don't know that they have the disease.

If you are the mother of a teenage daughter and she has unusually bad periods, it's wise to have a professional examine her. If you have been diagnosed yourself, you know how urgent it is to get treatment.

The Gynecological Exam for Teenagers

An internal exam can be embarrassing and stressful for anyone, particularly a teenager who is just coming to terms with her body and her need for privacy. Nonetheless, the exam is the only way a physician will be able to detect any congenital abnormality, rosary bead nodules, or pelvic mass that might be obstructing her menstrual flow.

Many teens with endometriosis have a malformation of the cervix, vagina, or uterus, which might contribute to retrograde menstruation. Others have an imperforate hymen that does not allow the passage of blood and menstrual debris out of the body. These abnormalities can be corrected surgically.

You can assure your daughter that the doctor's specula and other instruments are small and will leave her hymen intact. You and the doctor's nurse can be present at all times to support and comfort her.

Treatment for Teenagers

Although a sure diagnosis of endometriosis can be made only via laparoscopy, a surgical procedure is usually not the first step that would be taken for a young teenager. Your doctor will probably start you on anti-inflammatory drugs (Ansaid) or a prostaglandin inhibitor (Motrin or Anaprox). He will recommend that you begin taking the maximum daily dosage on the bottle before your period starts and continue until your flow has stopped. Because prostaglandin inhibitors slow or stop smooth muscle contraction, your menstrual cramps should improve.

If this treatment proves ineffective, your physician may prescribe a birth control pill to simulate pregnancy and stop your menstrual bleeding (see Chapter 6).

If neither medication is effective in reducing your pain or other symptoms, your doctor will probably recommend a laparoscopy and a tissue biopsy. This is the only way to prove that you do have endometriosis. It is also the only way to find out whether you have any other gynecological problems that should be treated. You may be put on a course of medication afterward—either Depo-Provera or danazol.

Most teenagers who have been treated for endometriosis have had excellent prognoses and follow-up exams. Early detection has proved very important in both immediate pain relief and later fertility.

OLDER WOMEN, PRE- AND POSTMENOPAUSAL

Adenomyosis

Adenomyosis is a disease that is often likened to endometriosis because it too involves tissue from the endometrium growing where it should not. But the two diseases are quite different. Whereas endo implants grow ectopically outside the uterus, adenomyosis occurs inside the uterine muscle. And whereas endo is typical of younger women, adenomyosis is typical of older women, either pre- or postmenopausal, usually those who have had children.

Women who've had endo don't usually contract adenomyosis in their later years. (The two have been reported to coexist in only 6 to 20 percent of all diagnosed cases.)

Some physicians feel that repeated childbearing may lead to adenomyosis. Repeated pregnancies may weaken the uterine walls, making them susceptible to the invasion of endometrial tissue through the muscle. Another possible cause is that many women with the disease have a naturally high estrogen level.

Your doctor may suspect adenomyosis if, during a bimanual exam, your uterus feels large and bulky with thickened walls. It may be greatly enlarged, as if you were ten or twelve weeks pregnant. You may have no symptoms at all, or you may feel extreme pain and tenderness in the uterus and experience heavy, abnormal bleeding.

Adenomyosis is extremely difficult to diagnose because there is no way to see the inside of the uterine muscle without removing the uterus. It is also hard to treat—there is currently no hormonal therapy for adenomyosis. Because it may present the possibility of a future malignancy, many physicians feel that the only way to treat it is to remove the uterus.

Why Should Endometriosis Proliferate after Menopause?

We know that endometriosis proliferates because of the bleeding and scarring pattern of the monthly cycle. If so, how can we explain the existence of endometriosis in women over fifty?

The reason is that the ovaries are not the only source of estrogen in the body. After menopause, the adrenal glands help to convert fat cells into a weakened form of estrogen known as *estrone.* So although a menopausal woman's monthly supply of ovarian estrogen has dried up, she still may have residual effects of pain and discomfort if her estrone levels are high.

Women with many fat cells tend to produce more estrone, so you have a higher chance of continuing endo symptoms if you are overweight.

The High Risk of Osteoporosis

One of the primary suspects in the endometriosis picture is immune-system deficiency (see Chapter 2). Women with endo tend to have more macrophages, or "clean-up" white blood cells, in their peritoneal fluid than women without endo. These macrophages secrete the hormone interleukin-1, which suppresses new bone growth. This means that women with endo also have a higher level of this hormone in their blood. They may have thinner bones and be at higher risk for osteoporosis.

Estrogen replacement therapy is often prescribed for women as a preventive measure against osteoporosis (see Chapter 8). But if your doctor has advised you not to take estrogen because of your endometriosis, there are other steps you can take to protect your bones.

- Your doctor may prescribe danazol or GnRH analogs. These drugs will stop your monthly cycling and consequently reduce the amount of estrogen in your body.

- You can maintain a daily regimen of weight-bearing exercise such as walking, jogging, aerobics, rowing, or bicycling.

- You can take additional calcium supplements or eat more calcium-rich foods.

- You can safety-proof your home to avoid accidents that might result in bone breaks. Tack down loose rugs and electrical cords. Repair the sidewalk outside your house if it needs it. Switch from high-heeled to flat shoes for everyday wear.

AGE IS NO PROTECTION AGAINST ENDOMETRIOSIS

Many teenagers and older women never see a doctor about their chronic symptoms because they believe that their age protects them from endometriosis. They may suffer in silence, and for no reason.

Whether you are thirteen or fifty-three, you *can* suffer from the symptoms of endometriosis. Regardless of your age, the sooner you seek a definite diagnosis and get into treatment, the sooner you can be assured of an active, pain-free existence.

ALTERNATIVE, COMPLEMENTARY TREATMENTS

Endometriosis can be managed only with expert, professional medical care. But many mysteries remain about the mechanisms of the disease, and medical science cannot at this time claim that any one technique or combination of techniques will offer complete relief. For this reason, many women choose to expand their treatment by using alternative, holistic therapies *in addition to traditional treatments* to attempt to ease pain and reduce stress in natural ways.

There is no hard, scientific evidence to explain why these methods would work, but many women are convinced of their effectiveness. And many physicians acknowledge that a combination of approaches to the disease, if complementary, can afford a well-rounded treatment regimen. If you are interested in exploring any of these alternative therapies, you should first discuss them thoroughly with your doctor and *use them only in conjunction with your regular medical treatment.*

PAIN MANAGEMENT

Pain is the undesirable but fairly constant companion of every woman who has endo. Although surgery and hormonal treatments reduce pain, for some women the pain that remains is intolerable. You don't have to tolerate excruciating agony—but you don't have to medicate it away either. It is not wise to use analgesics and narcotics continually over the many years you may have this chronic condition because of the dangers of tolerance and dependence. It's important for you to take the time and effort to learn new ways to coordinate your mind and body to regulate pain.

Many doctors feel that if you know what to do when you feel physically overwhelmed by your symptoms, you can reduce stress and actually reduce the pain. Many of the techniques described below have become invaluable additions to the conventional medical treatment of endometriosis.

Acupuncture

Acupuncture is a complex system of medicine that is based on energetics rather than biochemistry. Acupuncturists use superfine, disposable stainless-steel needles, which are manually twirled or stimulated with electric current on particular points in the body. The needles access into the body's natural energy. About five hundred of these points, located along twelve so-called meridians, have been identified in the body, although most acupuncturists use only about 150 in treatment.

The goal of acupuncture is not only to relieve pain and discomfort but to treat the condition that underlies the various symptoms. Many patients who try acupuncture for pain relief report a high degree of success. How can we explain this from a Western perspective? It's possible that the twirling needles trigger a release of endogenous opiates, which can relieve pain. It's also possible that the needles stimulate the production of antibodies, which fight infection. Although Western medicine has made great progress in exploring the electrical potential of the body, it is still not clear why acupuncture is so effective. But millions of people who've tried it swear that it is.

If you are treated by an acupuncturist for endometriosis, you will first be asked for a lengthy medical and personal case history. You will then be examined according to Chinese medicine. An examination of the tongue and the pulse can reveal the source of your problem to an acupuncturist.

The ancient Chinese philosophy underlying this system holds that each living thing is energized, or given life, by a combination of the opposites *yin* and *yang*—cold and hot, liquid and dry, feminine and masculine, dark and light. The life force, *ch'i*, can keep harmony only when the two are balanced. When the body is out of balance in any way, it can't function as it normally does, and problems can arise.

Think about endometriosis from this perspective. According to Chinese philosophy, *ch'i* must flow smoothly through the body to insure the passage of excess blood out of the body. If any of the body's meridians are blocked or congested, the blood (which is yang) and the *ch'i* (which is yin) will have difficulty moving properly. By moving the energy along the body's various meridians, balance can be reestablished between the two forces.

Needle stimulation will rush energy from a point on the hand or foot along the whole meridian through the organ that is affected. It will move any blockage that might exist along this path. The way the needle is inserted can make the energy in an organ stronger or pull excess energy out.

Chinese medicine believes that there are different patterns of endometriosis. If the *ch'i* is congested and the blood is "stagnant," there may be a deficiency of both *ch'i* and blood, or the body may be unnaturally cold or hot. Each of these patterns will cause a different set of endometriosis symptoms. Treatment would involve freeing up the *ch'i* and the blood and getting them back in balance.

Acupuncture can also be practiced simply to relieve pain. You may be able to find a medical doctor who has been trained in the use of acupuncture for pain relief. Western physicians have gotten excellent results by using needle stimulation to block the passage of the pain from nerve endings to the brain.

Finding a Qualified Acupuncturist

For a referral to an acupuncturist or to a pain-management center that uses acupuncture as part of its program, ask your doctor or contact a local university hospital or medical school. In many states, acupuncturists must be licensed to practice. If this is true in your state, you can ask your state medical board for their names.

It is essential that the acupuncturist you select always use completely sterilized techniques. All needles must be disposed of after use on one patient to guard against the spread of both hepatitis and AIDS.

Acupressure

The principles of acupressure are similar to those of acupuncture, but the practitioner uses directed finger-point stimulation to access into the body's medians.

Acupressure practitioners are on staff at pain clinics, or you may find one through a university hospital or medical school.

Transcutaneous Electrical
Nerve Stimulation (TENS)

In TENS treatment, a weak electrical current from a TENS machine is passed just under the surface of your skin near the site of your pain. As with acupuncture, no one is exactly sure how this technique works. One theory is that the stimulation of the electrodes blocks pain impulses from the afflicted organs to the brain. This may cause the release of a natural pain-killing substance into the blood and spinal fluid. Another theory is that the procedure shuts down the connection between the source of the pain and the pain-receiving center in the brain.

Many medical centers and university hospitals have the TENS machine, as do specialized pain clinics.

Biofeedback

The purpose of biofeedback is to teach you to use monitoring machines to alter functions in your body that are normally involuntary. A trained practitioner will show you how to use relaxation techniques in conjunction with information about your body's physical responses. By manipulating the signals you get from the biofeedback machine, you will learn to release muscle tension, lower your blood pressure and heart rate, and even change your temperature.

To master biofeedback training, you will need about ten sessions with a trainer. The trainer will teach you to work with the machines, and then you will practice at home. During your sessions, sensors running from a special machine are attached to your skin to measure your various bodily functions. By focusing mentally and physically, you can alter the readings on the machine. On the simplest level you can raise your blood pressure by thinking angry thoughts; you can lower it by imagining yourself in a quiet, lovely place with someone you like.

During the training, you learn how to manipulate these various bodily functions. Thinking of increased blood flow in your hands, for example, may allow you to divert blood flow away from your pelvic area.

One of the best uses of biofeedback is to reduce stress by learning to control those physical functions that are exacerbated by tension. This is particularly effective in the management of endometriosis symptoms, where physical and mental aspects can be inextricably intertwined.

Finding a Qualified Biofeedback Trainer

Your doctor may be able to recommend a qualified trainer, or you can get a local referral from the Biofeedback Society of America or the American Association of Biofeedback Clinicians (see Chapter 11).

Meditation

The goal of meditation is to empty the mind completely, which in turn will calm the body. When you meditate, you attempt to remove or reduce the impact of external stimuli by concentrating on a single point, usually a sound or an object.

People in a deeply meditative state have been found to be able to slow their pulse, lower their blood pressure, and decrease muscle tension. Although there is no hard scientific evidence that meditation is beneficial in the treatment of endo, it does reduce stress and allow you to clear and focus your energy on healing.

Meditation is usually part of yoga and tai ch'i classes. It can also be practiced in a course of transcendental meditation, or TM.

Imaging and Visualization

Various forms of relaxation exercises have proved very useful in the relief of endometriosis symptoms. These are based on a belief that the mind and body are one, and that by "changing your mind," you can also change your body.

Techniques such as visualization and imaging can help you empower yourself to mentally remove the source of pain or discomfort from your body. Some women imagine or visualize their adhesions melting or drying up; some imagine an army of white blood cells rushing to attack an endometrioma, which puts up no resistance and is destroyed, leaving a healthy ovary.

Another benefit of imaging is that it can distract you from unpleasant physical sensations. Simply recalling a scene in which you were particularly happy can take your mind off your pain.

Self-Hypnosis

Self-hypnosis is a form of meditation in which you put yourself into mental and physical state of calm and equanimity. In this state, you can give yourself suggestions about how you are going to deal with problems. You can suggest that your body is pushing the pain out or that your entire pelvic area is relaxed, like a calm lake on a windless day.

Although you can derive a certain benefit from being hypnotized by someone else, the only way to make this technique work for you all the time is to learn to do it for yourself.

Some psychiatrists and psychologists are trained in hypnotherapy. Ask your doctor or check with a local university hospital for a referral.

LIFE-STYLE MANAGEMENT

Nutritional Balance

It has not been medically proven that altering dietary intake improves endometriosis. Even so, many women with the condition have found that when they lower their fat, sugar, caffeine, and salt intake and eliminate processed and refined foods from their diet, they feel better.

It is important to have a healthy, well-balanced nutritional plan if you have endometriosis. Studies have shown that different enzymes in the body are affected by hormonal fluctuations. Some of the medications you take may interfere with your body's absorption of essential nutrients. Finally, eating well seems to energize most people and give them the vitality necessary for coping with chronic disease.

If you eat a good diet, you're getting most of your daily required vitamins. But women with endometriosis have a particular need for B-complex (the "antistress" vitamin, which also helps prevent fluid retention). Danazol has been shown to have an adverse effect on the body's supply of vitamin B_6, so you may want to consult your doctor or nutritionist about taking a supplement. Acidophilus, the "friendly" bacterium found in yogurt and available in capsule form, is excellent for digestive problems and can help restore the acid-base balance in a reproductive system that's been altered by hormonal changes. Vitamin E and selenium are often recommended to women with endo as emulsifiers in the blood.

Some women have gotten great relief from their endo symptoms by taking evening primrose oil, a food oil similar to saf-flower oil that contains a prostaglandin as a derivative element. Although it may seem contradictory to ingest something that is naturally responsible for much of endometriosis pain, anecdotal reports indicate that it has helped some women, perhaps by restoring the balance between the body's fatty acids and prostaglandins. Those who've noticed a relief of symptoms by taking the oil say that you should start with very small amounts and take it only with your doctor's consent.

Finding a Qualified Nutritionist

Professional nutritionists are aware of the various dietary needs of endo patients. University hospitals and medical schools are the best sources of referrals. You can also contact the American Dietetic Association or the Center for Science in the Public Interest (see Chapter 11).

The nutritionist will take a case history and conduct a variety of tests to determine your dietary needs. The first step will probably be to detoxify a body that's existed too long on processed foods, refined sugar, fats, and salts. The second step will be to give nutritional support and correct the imbalances that exist in your system.

The following easy principles are general guidelines to a good nutritional program.

- Cut down on saturated fats, salt, refined sugars, caffeine, processed foods, red meat, and alcohol.

- Eat more low-salt, low-cholesterol, high-fiber, high-carbohydrate foods.

- Eat smaller meals. It's preferable to have six small meals a day rather than three large ones.

- Don't experiment with radical diets. Just because someone tells you macrobiotics worked for her, this is no guarantee macrobiotics will do anything for you. Making huge changes in your dietary intake overnight can lead to gastrointestinal disturbances and nutritional deficiencies.

Exercise

Women with endometriosis often complain of fatigue and exhaustion. Their fatigue may result from a combination of physical and emotional elements. They are drained by dealing with their stress and pain and the uncertainty of whether they will ever be able to have a child.

One way to deal with fatigue effectively is to start a daily exercise program. The kind of exercise you do must be geared to your particular physical needs and abilities, and it should be practiced only with your doctor's supervision.

Exercise offers many different benefits to the endometriosis sufferer. A woman who feels terrible about having no control over her body can start to appreciate her body's amazing potential. Many daily exercisers swear that exercise is a "natural high." The physical basis for the temporary euphoria they are talking about is that exercising gives you a rush of adrenaline and releases endorphins, chemical substances produced in the brain that naturally make you feel good. Any kind of aerobic exercise—that is, something that raises your heartbeat and gets your lungs working—is going to give you this wonderful jolt of energy.

Exercise gets you moving, and you must compensate for the exertion you're under by taking in more oxygen. This is an additional benefit, because as you allow your lungs to expand, you are giving your body a way to use the energy stored within. Breathing deeply into your abdominal area and getting oxygen circulating around your reproductive organs seems to reduce pelvic pain in many women.

How to Choose an Appropriate Form of Exercise

Endometriosis adhesions often make bending and stretching difficult or impossible. For this reason, and particularly if you have just finished recuperating from surgery or are on a course of hormonal treatments, you should begin with the mildest form of exercise. It should cause no jarring motions that might pull on your adhesions. You may find that an activity that offers gentle stretching motions, both external and internal, is extremely helpful and relaxing.

Jogging, jumping rope, and high-impact aerobics are *not* appropriate for women with endometriosis. But other forms of weight-bearing exercise are recommended. Walking, biking, rowing, and low-impact aerobics are all suitable because they make use of repeated resistance against the body's own weight. This is extremely important for endo patients since it's been shown that they have a tendency to lose bone mass and may be at greater risk for osteoporosis. Although swimming is not weight-bearing, it is an excellent, soothing activity if you're in chronic pain.

For exercise to make a difference in your body and your outlook, you should do some form of it at least half an hour a day, five or six days a week. Start slowly so that you don't overexert yourself. If you stick with it, you'll build your stamina and frequency over time.

If you are about to begin an exercise program, always get your doctor's okay.

Wear the proper equipment—specifically good shoes and clothing that breathes. Get expert supervision to start with. An instructor at a health club is ideal.

If you feel pain or are short of breath, *stop exercising.* Pain indicates that you're doing something wrong.

No matter what form of exercise you choose, stick with it. You may make a few false starts before you find something that feels right for you. *Don't get discouraged* if you feel you aren't making progress and it isn't getting easier. It takes a long time to accustom your body to working out.

Meditative Exercise

Two types of meditative exercise that have been practiced for thousands of years offer inner calm and self-discipline. They are ideal for any woman with endometriosis because they also offer a new flexibility of body and spirit.

Yoga

Yoga is a series of postures, or *asanas,* that are held for different periods of time while the student works on breathing deeply and completely into all parts of her body. According to Indian thought, *prana* or "energy" is the power at the base of life. The practice of yoga keeps the *prana* in balance, which in turn keeps mind and body in balance.

Tai Ch'i

It is said that in the year A.D. 520 an Indian monk traveled to China in order to spread the Buddha's teachings. This began an intricate exchange of meditative and martial arts techniques between the two countries. In Chinese, *tai ch'i* means "the grand ultimate." The idea of being at the highest level, the most in tune with the cosmos, was developed as a method of manipulating an enemy by yielding rather than attacking. The word *ch'i* means nearly the same thing as *prana.* The purpose of the graceful *tai ch'i* exercises—performed in a set of 24, 48, 84, or 108 steps—is to move the energy that is stored throughout the body to promote health and longevity.

Massage

Massage may be the only "exercise" possible for women with endo who are in such pain that they cannot start a program of physical activity. Massage allows another person—a massage therapist, a practitioner at your health club, your spouse, or a friend—to help release tension from all your body parts. Some women report that they can feel their various internal organs respond favorably to the indirect healing effects of massage.

Sex Therapy

If you avoid sex because it is painful, but refuse to discuss it with your partner because the idea of confrontation is even more painful, you may need sex therapy.

A qualified sex therapist, particularly one familiar with the problems of couples suffering from dyspareunia (painful intercourse), can help you to reestablish bonds that were severed when your disease came between you. A therapist may have you explore your feelings about pain and sex, about pain and attempting to conceive a child, about guilt feelings of depriving each other of pleasure, and a variety of other problems associated with endometriosis. The therapist may suggest positions with the least penetration, different forms of nongenital lovemaking, or ways of being intimate without being sexual.

Your own doctor can probably recommend a licensed sex therapist familiar with the treatment of endometriosis. If not, a sex therapy program associated with a teaching hospital is a good source of referrals.

Behavior Modification

The goal of behavior modification is to substitute positive behaviors for negative or maladaptive behaviors. According to behaviorist theory, all our behavior is learned, including our ability to deal with pain. We tend to repeat behaviors for which we are rewarded and avoid behaviors that cause us distress or for which we get negative reinforcement. If we change our behavior, we can handle pain better.

A behavioral therapist will counsel you to examine your endometriosis patterns and "unlearn" your typical responses to pain and discomfort. If you always take to your bed three days before your period starts, if you avoid sex or cancel appointments, you are expecting pain to make you dysfunctional. You might alter this behavior if you had something special to look forward to—like a night at the theater or an enjoyable meal.

It is not easy to change behavior at first, but when you understand the process and begin rewarding yourself for positive rather than negative reactions, you gain more control over your life.

Your own doctor may recommend a behavioral therapist, or you may find one by contacting the American Association for the Advancement of Behavior Therapy (see Chapter 11).

Homeopathy

Homeopathy is practiced by medical doctors who treat illness based on the "law of similars." That is, they believe that illnesses can be treated by introducing trace elements of toxic substances that create symptoms *similar to* the symptoms of the illness. Though the toxin would make a healthy person sick, it has the reverse effect on someone who is already sick.

Substances used in homeopathic treatment include aconite,

arsenic, sulphur, ipecac—and about four hundred others. Minute doses of these toxins are taken alone, or in combination, corresponding to particular illnesses. (Traditional Western medicine—*allopathic* treatment—uses drugs or surgery to treat disease, based on the belief that an outside agent can produce healthful results *opposite to* the symptoms of sickness.)

Homeopathy also involves a belief that mind and body are inseparable and that whatever condition affects the body is caused by a problem in the psyche.

If you have endo and are treated by a homeopathic physician, he or she would do a lengthy—perhaps two-hour—case history on you. The doctor will want to know all about your family background and your childhood; any other diseases you might have had; and how endometriosis affects your daily life, your sleep, your work, and your relationship with your family. You might be given homeopathic medicine or counseling or both during your sessions.

If you are currently under the care of a traditional allopathic physician, he or she must remain your primary medical adviser. You should not wean yourself off hormonal treatment or delay surgery unless you have discussed the possible ramifications with both your allopathic and your homeopathic health-care providers.

Finding a Homeopathic Doctor

Homeopathic practitioners are medical doctors and must be licensed by the state to practice, so your state medical board can give you a list of the ones in your area. You may wish to consult with a few before you make a selection. It's also a good idea to ask to speak with several of each doctor's endometriosis patients about the diagnosis and treatment they received.

Chiropractic

Chiropractic is the manual manipulation of the vertebrae in the spinal column with the intention of balancing nerve energy in the body. Since the nervous system is couched within the spinal column, the chiropractor manipulates the lower back to stimulate the nerves that go to the uterus and ovaries. The system is cross-protected—that is, if you cut a nerve that goes directly into the uterus, another at a different vertebral level will take over its function.

A chiropractor will probably do a series of X rays to look directly at your vertebrae and will do a physical history and exam to see what your neurological needs might be. He or she may use ultrasound to locate the various areas that are affected and that may be directly or indirectly causing pain and related symptoms.

Be extremely wary of practitioners who use aggressive physical force with vertebral manipulations. Chiropractic, if improperly done, can cause spinal cord problems. You should also be wary of agreeing to continue therapy without a cut-off date. A course of chiropractic can last for months, but it should not go on indefinitely. Most insurance companies now cover reasonable periods of treatment.

Chiropractors must be licensed by the state in which they practice. You can contact your state licensing board for a referral, or write to the American Chiropractic Association for a list of qualified doctors of chiropractic in your area (see Chapter 11).

A Holistic Approach to the Body

Most practitioners of these alternative treatments believe that the mind and body must be treated together, as one organism, and that illness may result from an imbalance of the two. You can't correct your imbalances overnight, and the longer you've suffered from endometriosis, the longer the correction will take. This doesn't mean, however, that you can't find a great deal of relief and energy in the course of your treatment.

But because there are still so many unknowns related to this chronic condition, it is essential that you continue your allopathic treatments. You can benefit greatly from nutritional balance, exercise, biofeedback, or meditation, but you must have proper medical management at the same time. The point is to alleviate as much discomfort and make yourself feel as good—physically, mentally, and emotionally—as you possibly can.

ELEVEN

WHERE TO GO FOR HELP

If you have endometriosis, you have a chronic disease. It will probably require careful management throughout your life. Though enormous advances in the study, diagnosis, and treatment of endometriosis have been made over the last ten years, there is still no cure. This means that you, as an informed medical consumer, owe it to yourself to use every resource at your disposal to get as much help as you can.

A library in a good-size city is your first best source of research and information. Most university and hospital libraries allow the public to have access to their books and medical research services, although some may charge a fee for use.

You can investigate a variety of specialized organizations and allied support and self-help groups.

The development of the Endometriosis Association, an international organization, has made it possible for women and their physicians to be aware of the disease and to understand many more of its ramifications. The association advocates research and keeps its members up to date on the latest news on hormonal, surgical, and alternative therapies.

Endometriosis Association
U.S.–Canada Headquarters
8585 North 76th Place
Milwaukee WI 53223
    1-800-992-ENDO (U.S.)
    1-800-426-2END (Canada)

It has chapters in every state and abroad and encourages the growth of local support groups for women to get together and talk about their failures and successes, to share information about doctors and treatment, and most important, to offer each other hope.

If you want an information packet or have any questions about your symptoms, diagnosis, or treatment, use the hot-line "800" numbers.

ENDOMETRIOSIS TREATMENT

Hundreds of private physicians treat endometriosis and infertility around the country. It's best to select a physician close to you because managing this disease requires frequent contact with your health-care provider. There are, however, a handful of specialists who have made innovative strides in the field. Even if you don't live within commuting distance, you may wish to consult one of these doctors about your current or future treatment.

Camran Nezhat, M.D.
Fertility and Endocrinology Center
5555 Peachtree Dunwoody Road, N.E.
Atlanta GA 30342
    (404) 255-8778

W. Paul Dmowski, M.D.
Institute for the Study and Treatment of Endometriosis
Grant Hospital
550 West Webster
Chicago IL 60614
 (312) 883-3881

Lyle Breitkopf, M.D., and Robert Breitstein, M.D.
Beekman Downtown Hospital
170 William Street
New York NY 10002
 (212) 312-5000

The Beekman is the only public clinic for the treatment of endometriosis. Both physicians donate their time. A psychologist who runs support groups is also on staff to talk with patients. Drs. Breitkopf and Breitstein also see patients in their private practice:

333 East 57th Street
New York NY 10022
 (212) 486-2222

Another innovative specialist is:

David Redwine, M.D.
St. Charles Medical Center
2500 N.E. Neff Road
Bend OR 97701
 (503) 382-4321

This is one of the few facilities that specializes in the treatment of teenagers with endometriosis:

Donald Goldstein, M.D.
Boston Children's Hospital Medical Center
300 Longwood Avenue
Boston MA 02015
 (617) 735-7648

PAIN MANAGEMENT

Because pain is a complex and difficult topic, you should do all you can to inform yourself about how the mechanisms of pain work and what you can do to alleviate pain. The following groups may send you brochures on proven techniques or provide referrals to pain management clinics near you:

American Society of Anesthesiologists
515 Busse Parkway
Park Ridge IL 60068
   (312) 332-6360

American Pain Society
P.O. Box 186
Skokie IL 60076
   (312) 475-1000

American Chronic Pain Association
257 Old Haymaker
Monroeville PA 15146
   (412) 856-9676

This information-gathering organization is responsible for the development of the endometriosis point system. It can provide you with booklets and information sheets about infertility:

American Fertility Society
2131 Magnolia Avenue, Suite 201
Birmingham AL 35256-6199
   (205) 251-9764

HOMEOPATHY

Homeopathic doctors treat patients by the "law of similars," believing that a small dose of a toxin that makes well people sick has the reverse effect on someone who is sick. For general information, fact sheets, and listings of licensed practitioners in your area, contact:

International Foundation for Homeopathy
2366 East Lake E., 301
Seattle WA 98102
   (206) 324-8230

National Center for Homeopathy
1500 Massachusetts Avenue, N.W.
Washington DC 20005
   (202) 223-6182

SELF-HYPNOSIS

Self-hypnosis is a proven technique for dealing with pain. If you are interested in learning to use this alternative therapy, contact the following organizations for general information, fact sheets, and listings of licensed practitioners in your area.

American Association of Professional Hypnotherapists
P.O. Box 731
McLean VA 22101
   (703) 448-9623

American Society of Clinical Hypnosis
2250 East Devon Avenue, Suite 336
Des Plaines IL 60018
   (312) 297-3317

CHIROPRACTIC

Chiropractic physicians believe that manipulation of the spine can affect the nervous system and therefore the entire body. For information about chiropractic and a list of doctors of chiropractic in your area, contact:

American Chiropractic Association
1091 Wilson Boulevard
Arlington VA 22201
    (703) 276-8800

BIOFEEDBACK

Biofeedback training teaches you to control involuntary bodily functions such as temperature, blood pressure, and muscle tension for relief of pain. If you want information about the technique or are interested in lists of practitioners, hospitals, and pain management centers that use biofeedback, contact:

American Association of Biofeedback Clinicians
2424 South Demptster Avenue
Des Plaines IL 60016
    (312) 827-0440

PSYCHOTHERAPY AND SEX THERAPY

This is a huge field, and you must pick carefully from among its practitioners. A psychiatrist must have a medical degree; a psychologist must have a doctor of psychology degree. A sex therapist must have specialized training in the physical and emotional elements of sexual dysfunction. A "therapist" or "counselor" of any persuasion may be certified but does not have to be licensed.

Be sure to do some reading about the different psychotherapeutic methods and philosophies before trying to select a therapist who's right for you.

American Association for the Advancement
of Behavior Therapy
420 Lexington Avenue
New York NY 10170
(212) 682-0065

American Psychiatric Association
1700 18th Street, N.W.
Washington DC 20009
(202) 797-4900

American Psychological Association
1200 17th Street, N.W.
Washington DC 20036
(202) 833-7600

American Association of Sex Educators,
Counselors and Therapists
11 Dupont Circle
Washington DC 20036
(202) 462-1171

National Clearinghouse for Mental Health Information
Public Inquiries Section
5600 Fishers Lane, Room 11A-21
Rockville MD 20857
(301) 443-4513

WOMEN'S HEALTH CARE

For general information about endometriosis and a listing of physicians in your area who specialize in treatment of the disease, contact:

American College of Obstetricians and Gynecologists
600 Maryland Avenue, S.W.
Washington DC 10014
(202) 638-5577

GENERAL MEDICAL RESEARCH

This organization will do research for you on standard or alternative therapies currently in use for any disease or condition. For a $40 fee, it offers either a computer search on conventional medical treatments or a library search on alternative therapies.

World Research Foundation, California
15300 Ventura Boulevard, Suite 405
Sherman Oaks CA 91403
(818) 907-5483

RECOMMENDED READING

Ballweg, Mary Lou, and the Endometriosis Association. *Overcoming Endometriosis.* Congdon and Weed, 1987.

Breitkopf, Lyle. *Coping with Endometriosis.* Englewood Cliffs, N.J.: Prentice-Hall, 1987.

Older, Julia. *Endometriosis.* New York: Charles Scribner's Sons, 1984.

Schenken, Robert S. *Endometriosis: Contemporary Concepts in Clinical Management.* Textbook available from the Endometriosis Association, Milwaukee, Wis.

Weinstein, Kate. *Living with Endometriosis.* Reading, Mass.: Addison-Wesley, 1987.

Wilson, Emery. *Endometriosis.* Textbook available from the Endometriosis Association, Milwaukee, Wis.

GLOSSARY

adenomyosis: a condition of older women, either pre- or post-menopausal, in which cells from the endometrium invade the uterine wall, causing a tender, enlarged uterus. Severe cases may require a hysterectomy.

adhesion: a fibrous or weblike band of tissue that binds organs together. May be caused by endometrial implants or by scar tissue from previous operations.

adrenal gland: an endocrine-producing gland above each kidney that secretes androgens (testosterone).

androgen: a hormone responsible for male sex characteristics; specifically, testosterone.

antibody: a part of the body's immune system. A fighting cell that attacks a specific target.

antigen: any substance that can cause the formation of antibodies. The antigen is like a flag that signals the antibody's attack.

autoimmune deficiency: the body's lack of ability to fight off invading foreign cells.

barium enema: the injection of barium through a tube inserted into the rectum so that the doctor can take an X ray and do a fluoroscopic examination of the intestines.

benign: not malignant (cancerous).

biopsy: a removal of tissue for microscopic examination.

candidiasis: an infection caused by a yeastlike fungus.

cauterization: the destruction of tissue with heat.

cervix: the rounded, cone-shaped neck of the uterus, about an inch long. Part of it protrudes into the vagina.

chlamydia: a sexually transmitted disease of the cervix. If untreated, the resulting infection can lead to PID.

chocolate cyst: an endometrioma. A large benign tumor of endometrial tissue, filled with old blood, that usually grows on the ovaries.

cilia: hairlike projections from the epithelial cells, such as those lining the fallopian tubes.

clomiphene citrate (Clomid): an estrogen analog used to induce ovulation. A drug for the treatment of infertility.

cul-de-sac: a fold of the peritoneum that forms a pouch between the uterus and the rectum. Often a site of endometriosis.

danazol: a testosterone derivative that suppresses the release of FSH and LH, producing a pseudomenopause. The drug can have masculinizing side effects. It is commonly used in the treatment of endometriosis. Sold as Danocrine.

Depo-Provera: the injectable form of progesterone used to treat endometriosis.

dysmenorrhea: painful menses.

dyspareunia: painful intercourse.

ectopic: misplaced. In endometriosis any endometrial cells growing outside the uterus are ectopic.

endometrial biopsy: a diagnostic procedure performed by inserting an instrument through the cervix into the uterus to get a sample of the endometrial lining.

endometrioma: see *chocolate cyst.*

endometrium: the mucous membrane that lines the uterus. It is shed each month as menstrual bleeding.

estrogen: a hormone released by the follicles in the ovary as they mature. Endometrial implants swell and bleed each month under the influence of estrogen.

fallopian tubes: the tubes or ducts that extend from either end of the uterus. They convey the egg from the ovary to the uterus during each monthly cycle. A common site for endometriosis.

fiber optic: an instrument made of glass fibers that conducts light. The KTP laser used to treat endometriosis uses fiber optics.

fimbria: the fingerlike projections at the top of the fallopian tubes.

FSH (follicle-stimulating hormone): a hormone secreted by the pituitary gland that helps trigger the release of estrogen and progesterone by the ovaries.

GIFT (gamete intrafallopian transfer): a technique of artificial insemination used for infertile women who have one tube and ovary intact. In this procedure ova are retrieved from the body, mixed with sperm, and reinserted at the opening of the fallopian tube through a laparoscope.

GnRH (gonadotrophin-releasing hormone): a hormone naturally released in a pulsing fashion by the hypothalamus. It triggers the menstrual cycle.

GnRH analog: a man-made version of the hormone used in the treatment of endometriosis. By giving the analog continuously, the hormonal cycle is downregulated. The effect on the body is a pseudomenopause.

gonorrhea: a sexually transmitted disease of the cervix, rectum, and urethra. If untreated, it can lead to PID.

hormone: a chemical messenger produced by the endocrine glands. Travels through the body by means of the circulatory and lymphatic systems.

hymen: a thin mucous membrane across the lower opening of the vagina. An *imperforate hymen* is one that allows no natural outlet for menstrual debris.

hysterectomy: the surgical removal of the uterus and cervix.

Known as radical surgery. Sometimes used to treat endometriosis.

hysterosalpingogram: a diagnostic procedure used to determine whether the fallopian tubes are blocked. An X ray is taken while dye is injected into the uterus. The doctor is able to see whether the dye passes through the tubes.

iatrogenic: resulting from medical or surgical treatment, as scar tissue that grows postoperatively.

implant: an island of endometriosis tissue.

infertility: the state of being unable to conceive a child after one year of unprotected sexual activity.

IVF (in vitro fertilization): a technique of artificial insemination used for infertile women who have only a piece of an ovary intact. Ova are retrieved from the body and fertilized by sperm in a petrie dish. After the cells have begun to develop, they are reinserted into the uterus.

laparoscopy: a diagnostic procedure and treatment for endometriosis, also known as *bellybutton surgery.* A viewing instrument is inserted into the abdominal cavity so that the surgeon can identify endometrial implants. He may decide to remove them during the procedure by scalpel, laser, or cautery.

laparotomy: major abdominal surgery in which an incision is made along the pubic hairline so that the surgeon can laser, cut, or cauterize large endometriomas and adhesions.

laser surgery: the use of a highly concentrated beam of light to cut tissue.

LH (luteinizing hormone): one of the pituitary hormones that influence ovulation.

lymphatic system: a system of drainage and cleaning vessels running throughout the body. This system is part of the body's defense against infection and disease. It is thought that endometriosis may be spread through this system.

macrophage: a "scavenger" cell—a white blood cell that acts as a cleansing agent in the blood. Women with endometriosis tend to have an overabundance of these cells.

menopause: the end of a woman's reproductive capacity, marked by her last menstrual period.

menstruation: the monthly flow of blood, cervical mucus, and endometrial tissue down through the uterus and out the vagina.

microsurgery: surgery performed with the use of microscopes and magnifying lenses, often through a laparoscope.

nodule: a small, firm lump or mass that the doctor can feel during an internal exam.

oophorectomy (ovariectomy): the surgical removal of ovaries.

osteoporosis: literally, "porous bones." A condition resulting from estrogen depletion. A woman who has had her ovaries removed for treatment of chronic endometriosis may be at high risk for this disease. It can be treated with hormone replacement or other medication.

ovarian wedge resection: removal of part of the ovary or ovaries.

ovary: one of two almond-shaped glands in the female body that contain eggs. It produces the two hormones estrogen and progesterone.

ovulation: the monthly ripening and rupture of the egg from its follicle.

patent: open or unblocked, as the fallopian tubes.

peritoneal fluid: fluid made by the peritoneum.

peritoneum: "Saran-wrap" lining of the abdominal cavity. Often a site of endometriosis implants.

pelviscopic surgery: a relatively new and not widely available type of pelvic surgery, harsher than a laparoscopy. The equipment has the capacity to chop up large tumors or cysts and remove them from the body through the pelviscope.

PID (pelvic inflammatory disease): any inflammation of

the female reproductive system. Its symptoms are often confused with those of endometriosis.

postcoital test: an analysis of vaginal and cervical secretions performed a few hours after sexual intercourse.

presacral neurectomy: the cutting of the nerves in back of the uterus for pain relief in the treatment of endometriosis.

progestogen (progestin): the synthetic form of the hormone progesterone. Sometimes used in the treatment of endometriosis.

progesterone: a hormone produced during the second half of the menstrual cycle. It is responsible for thickening the endometrial lining as a possible home for an implanted egg. It therefore helps nourish endometriosis implants.

prostaglandins: fatty-acid derivatives with hormonelike qualities. They stimulate contraction of the smooth muscles. Dysmenorrhea in women with endo may result from an overabundance of them.

rectum: the lowest part of the large intestine. Often a site of endometriosis implants.

retrograde (reflux) menstruation: a prevalent theory of the cause of endometriosis. Holds that some menstrual blood backs up each month through the fallopian tubes and into the pelvic cavity.

stroma: the part of an endometrial implant or cyst that bleeds.

TAHBSO (total abdominal hysterectomy and bilateral salpingo-oophorectomy): removal of all reproductive organs, including uterus, cervix, fallopian tubes, and ovaries. Also known as a "clean-out."

tuboplasty: the reconstruction of a fallopian tube using microsurgery.

ultrasound: a technique that bounces high-frequency sound waves off soft tissue in the body to produce a picture on a screen. The procedure is helpful in determining the location of a mass, although it cannot identify the type of mass.

ureter: the tube that drains urine from the kidneys.

urethra: the channel leading from the bladder to outside the body.

uterine suspension: a tightening and shortening of the uterine ligaments. Often performed on endometriosis patients to draw the uterus up and out of the way.

uterosacral neurectomy: the cutting of the ligaments in back of the uterus. For relief of pain in endometriosis treatment.

uterus: a pear-shaped muscular organ lined with the endometrium. Its function is to nourish and house the embryo and fetus from implantation to birth. It is also a site of hormonal activity and sexual pleasure.

vagina: the canal that runs from the external genitalia inward to the cervix.

INDEX

Note: Endometriosis is abbreviated as "endo" throughout the index.

ABOUT THE AUTHOR

Judith Sachs was born in New York City, the daughter and granddaughter of physicians. Among her other nonfiction titles are *What Women Should Know About Menopause* (Dell Medical Library Series); *The Anxious Parent,* with Dr. Michael Schwartzman (Simon & Schuster); and *After the Fast,* with Dr. Phillip Sinaikin (Doubleday). She has also written a novel, *Honor the Dream* (Pocket Books) about the doctor/patient relationship in turn-of-the-century America. She lives in Pennington, New Jersey, with her husband and daughter, where she is working on a book about diet and longevity.